WORLD HISTORY

THE BASICS

'This is an engaging as well as much-needed introduction. It will be of great value to both instructors and students working in the field of world history.'

Marc Jason Gilbert, *Hawaii Pacific University*

World history has rapidly grown to become one of the most popular and talked about approaches to the study of history. *World History The Basics* introduces this fast-growing field and addresses key questions such as:

- What is world history?
- How do we study a subject with such a broad geographic and chronological range?
- Why has world history been controversial?

Written by one of the founders of the field and addressing all of the major issues including time, place, civilizations, contact, themes and more, this book is both an ideal introduction to world history and an important statement about the past, present and future of the field.

Peter N. Stearns is Provost and Professor of History at George Mason University. He is series editor for Routledge's Themes in World History and founder and editor of the *Journal of Social History*.

The Basics

WORLD HISTORY

THE BASICS

Peter N. Stearns

Routledge
Taylor & Francis Group

LONDON AND NEW YORK

For Aidan, Chloe and Inanna, who will live through
much world history

First published 2011
by Routledge
2 Park Square, Milton Park, Abingdon, Oxon OX14 4RN

Simultaneously published in the USA and Canada
by Routledge
270 Madison Avenue, New York, NY 10016

Routledge is an imprint of the Taylor & Francis Group, an informa business

© 2011 Peter N. Stearns
The right of Peter N. Stearns to be identified as author of this work has been
asserted by him in accordance with sections 77 and 78 of the Copyright, Designs and
Patents Act 1988.

Typeset in Aldus by Taylor & Francis Books
Printed and bound in Great Britain by TJ International, Padstow, Cornwall

British Library Cataloguing in Publication Data
A catalogue record for this book is available from the British Library

Library of Congress Cataloging in Publication Data
Stearns, Peter N.
World history : the basics / Peter N. Stearns.
    p. cm.
1. World history. 2. History–Philosophy.
3. History–Study and teaching. I. Title.
D16.8.S737 2010
909–dc22
2010018497

ISBN 13: 978-0-415-58274-2 (hbk)
ISBN 13: 978-0-415-58275-9 (pbk)
ISBN 13: 978-0-203-83994-2 (ebk)

CONTENTS

ACKNOWLEDGMENTS

I am deeply grateful to Laura Bell and Clio Stearns for various assistance in preparing this book, and for much good cheer. My thanks also to the world history students I've had the pleasure of working with at George Mason; they have taught me a great deal.

INTRODUCTION

WHAT AND *WHY* IS WORLD HISTORY?

The most important point to know about any subject, when beginning to engage with it, is: what's the purpose; why bother?

The basic reason to study world history involves access to the historical context for the globalized society we live in today (whether one likes a globalized society or not). Correspondingly, the reasons world history courses and programs have soared over the past quarter-century in the United States but also a number of other places, are that more and more educators, and students, have realized how complex and interconnected the world they live in has become, and have identified the resulting need for a new kind of historical scope. Purely national or regional histories no longer do the trick, though they may be exceptionally useful alongside a world history approach. We need a history that shows how world relationships have emerged and how different cultural and political traditions have formed and interacted. That's what the world is about now, and that's what world history can help explain.

This said, there are some supporting rationales, though they are much less important than the primary claim. A decisive factor in creating American interest in world history, from both high schools and colleges-universities, was the growing diversity of the student body. With more students arriving from backgrounds in Africa, Asia and Latin America, and often also with greater interest in their heritage, the need to offer a history that went beyond purely American or West European content became compelling. This was one reason world history initially spread more rapidly, as a teaching subject, at state colleges than at the elite private institutions whose enrollments were less mixed. But there were outright student protests at places like Stanford, pressing for more innovation in the history curriculum instead of a purely Western diet, and these currents unquestionably opened new doors for the world approach.

World history offers genuine new discoveries, a third reason to move it forward as a subject area. We will see that additions are particularly telling for the periods 600–1450 and 1450–1750, where escaping a narrow Western framework is particularly refreshing (even, it can be argued, for a proper understanding of the West itself). But world history adds new data and new points of view to virtually every period, even the great age of Western imperialism in the nineteenth century. New stories are available, new reasons to become intrigued with the past. Above all, new vantage points emerge that clarify what the past was all about and how it relates to the present. Most world historians would argue that in the process a more accurate view of the past emerges, and accuracy is not to be scorned.

This returns us to the main points: world history fosters methods of analysis that prepare people at all levels to deal with the issues that contemporary global society poses, and will pose in the future.

All this assumes that world history can deliver on its promises. The goal of providing the mixture of facts, skills and analyses that meet the demanding criterion of using the past to explain the global present is undeniably challenging. Students in world history courses should be able to say, at the end of their labors, that they've at least made serious advances in that direction.

WORLD HISTORY AS CONTROVERSY

The reasons for world history seem so obvious to most world historians, and to many students as well, that it may seem odd that there have been serious battles about the subject and that many countries reject the whole approach even today. In the United States, world history played a significant role in what many people called the "culture wars" of the 1990s, and while the dust has settled a bit, too much emphasis on world history can still stir up storms in some quarters. In other countries, particularly where history teaching is more separate from history scholarship than is true in the United States, references to world history can also rouse major controversies.

In 1994, in fact, the United States Senate voted 99–1 against a world history plan for high schools that had been designed by a large committee of university historians and high school history teachers. The Senate was admittedly moved by a recent election which had returned a large conservative Republican majority. It was also reacting to a parallel plan for United States history that generated even more dismay, because it seemed to depart from established norms. But the concern about world history itself was genuine, for it is rare that an academic subject rouses that much disapproval from the senior legislative body in a whole nation.

The Senate was perturbed that world history seemed to downgrade any special qualities for Western civilization, which was in turn seen as the progenitor of key cultural and political themes in the United States. Its resolution intoned that any national history project "should have a decent respect for the traditions of Western civilization." Without question, as we will see, world history does compete with earlier courses in European history or "western civ," and without question world history does tend to regard the Western case as one among several rather than possessed of clearly special virtues. Western civilization courses, in contrast, had gained traction in the United States partly because they allowed emphasis on particular qualities Americans might hold dear (like real or imagined Renaissance individualism). While the Senate did not exactly say that world history was wrongheaded, its resolution clearly sought at the very least to single out a special place for Western values.

The Senate resolution did not cut off the world history movement in the United States, and indeed barely influenced it. Most states, in fact, as they developed history standards used a world history rubric from the mid-1990s onward. But closer examination revealed a host of problems unresolved. Most state standards and the kinds of textbooks used in high school world history courses, continued to give disproportionate attention to the West (to the tune of an average 67% of text coverage). This led world historians to complain that the resultant courses, often derisively labeled "the West and the rest," seriously distorted what world history should really be about. Even as the world history label gained ground, the United States government promoted a massive "Teach American History" movement, with unprecedented federal funding, that while not explicitly hostile to world history implicitly made it clear that the national history was what was really important. Even the crisis following the terrorist attacks of 9/11/2001 generated signs of the ongoing division. While many educators and much of the general public saw the attacks as a sign that Americans should learn more about other parts of the world, including Islam, conservative spokespeople urged that this was the time to circle the wagons around the study of (and praise for) Western history.

The basic debate, which we will see repeated in virtually every region and resolved almost nowhere, really focused on the purpose of history, and the American hesitation about Western civ was merely a variant. Most countries, in the past two centuries, have looked to history education primarily to instill an agreed-upon national story and (usually) a set of implied national strengths. History was central, in other words, to identity formation and political orthodoxy. A sophisticated course might, to be sure, admit an occasional national mistake – like the United States treatment of Native Americans, or slavery – but this should be overridden by emphasis on the positive.

In the case of the United States, with a relatively short history, this national focus was supplemented by the Western civ backdrop. High schools and colleges from the 1920s onward frequently introduced a European course alongside an American history requirement, so that students might emerge with a strong sense of the national story bolstered by at least some understanding that national merits were further justified by their link to a longer and largely uplifting Western backdrop.

World history, quite simply, takes a different tack. It does not necessarily dispute the national or national-with-civilizational approach – world historians have not usually argued that we should abolish the teaching of American history, though some would like that history to be considerably revised – but it definitely touts a different set of goals at least for the world course. World history need not attack national identities, but it does not see support for these identities to be a key purpose at least of this part of a history program. The goal, again, is understanding global conditions through a historical lens. This in turn involves some serious attention to several major cultural traditions, and not just one's own. Understanding global conditions also involves careful exploration of contacts among different societies and to larger forces – like trade patterns, or exchange of technologies – that help shape the experience of any particular region. World historians argue that these central concerns – comparative attention to several distinct cultural and political experiences and a focus on factors that transcend single societies are the key components of any historical understanding of the world we live in. But they also strongly imply, if they do not say outright, that a purely national or regional lens cannot possibly capture this same world.

And this is the central dispute. Most societies in the world today, and not just the United States, continue to bring a deeply national commitment to history teaching – even when the same societies generate historical research that is less confined. For many, recent developments have heightened the national or regional focus. Russia, for example, had urgent needs to reexamine its school history programs after the fall of communism in 1991, and great attention has been paid to innovation – but almost entirely within a national context. The European Union has been attempting to promote history teaching that will emphasize Europe's common bonds – and while this project is not anti-global, it does not place any premium on wider or non-European developments, and it can generate nervousness about too much global detraction.

Even besides specific new needs, the larger force of contemporary globalization inevitably produces a divided history response – which is precisely what the American culture wars are all about. World historians look at developments around us and argue that they clearly point to the need to take the widest possible view, to pay attention to a number of societies besides one's own and to the evolution of patterns of trade or migration that have long affected any individual regional experience. But many people, including many educators and politicians, look at the same developments around us and argue that they point to an urgent need to shore up the national tradition. The very processes of globalization that intrigue world historians – though they may be very critical of certain features – cause grave concern for lots of publics. In fact, international opinion polls show that cultural globalization – the outside influences that impinge on regional beliefs and values – is the most feared aspect of the whole situation; 72% of those polled around the world profess to be against this aspect, whereas only 56% say they fear economic globalization. And if cultural globalization is an enemy, what more logical way to react than to try to reassert the storied qualities of the national history story?

The larger pressures of globalization surely also help explain tense debates in Australia. Here, the federal government launched a major program in 2000 to improve the teaching of history in the schools, and while much attention focused on local history the program also insisted on knowledge of global events and issues. The result prompted significant backlash, with new pride in Australia's history at virtually all educational levels. A number of critics reported their shock that some students knew about World War II and Stalinism but not the name of Australia's first prime minister. Arguments of this sort have unfolded virtually in any country where even timid gestures toward world history have surfaced. The same arguments explain why many countries, with sophisticated history enterprises in other respects, have not moved toward world history significantly at all.

In the current moment, in sum, world history is inevitably the subject of real controversy, even if most countries (unlike the United States in 1994) keep the subject out of the halls of parliament. World history is an innovation, a deliberate departure from the way history has usually been framed at least at the teaching level. Its justifications do not focus on instilling national identity or patriotic loyalty – though they do not inevitably contradict such purposes. Its goals assume that students should learn something about several identities and related cultures, and not just one, and also something about global interactions that go beyond regional identities of any sort. These are not subversive goals, but they do challenge established history routines and they make some people anxious.

HOW WORLD HISTORY EMERGED

World history is both very old and very new. Many historians, in many societies, tried to take a large view of the world when they wrote their histories. Herodotus, in fifth-century Athens, authored a mixture of history, travelogue and fantasy about a variety of places he visited around the eastern Mediterranean – this in contrast to a slightly later classical Greek historian, Thucydides, who focused rigorously on Greece and its city states, and nothing really beyond. The great Arab historian, the North African Ibn Khaldun, also tried to keep many parts of the world in mind. In eighteenth-century Europe, a variety of Enlightenment intellectuals, including Voltaire, wrote histories that were not narrowly confined to Western Europe. None of these historians was, by contemporary standards, a full world historian, simply because not enough was known about several different parts of the world for them to be really inclusive. But their goal was wide ranging, if not literally global, and it would have been logical to expect, with the rise of more formal historical study, to see a fuller world history emerge without too much difficulty.

The nineteenth century, and its fascination with nationalism, seriously disrupted what might otherwise have been a reasonably natural trend. Historical work expanded, and increasingly history began to be included in school curricula in Europe and the United States, but the focus rested heavily on the national experience. To be sure, in many cases, the purely national interest was leavened by some attention to the history of ancient Greece and Rome and, in the United States, in European history more generally – but as we have seen these latter engagements usually formed a backdrop to the national story.

The narrowing of the history mission was further enhanced by another nineteenth-century development, worthy in its own right: a growing interest in a heavily fact-based, elaborately researched scholarly presentation. Beginning in Germany with the great historian Leopold von Ranke, a new effort to make history more professional and precise involved insistence on portraying the past "as it actually was." Translated into historical practice, this meant increasing attention to detailed archival research, producing often long, heavily footnoted books that provided a great deal of information about specific topics. At the hands of a master – like the nineteenth-century Swiss historian, Jacob Burckhardt, who wrote a classic study of the Italian Renaissance – this new approach could produce a lasting characterization of a significant historical period or episode. On the whole, however, the new historical precision encouraged a choice of somewhat more limited topics, like a specific war, or treaty, or presidency. Most contemporary historians still appreciate the impulses behind this professional turn: we want our histories to be as accurate as possible and to rest on careful research. It is true, however, that translating this approach into world history is a real challenge, particularly for younger scholars, simply because it's hard to generate that level of detail and that definite a research base when dealing with more than one major society or with such a vast topic as, say, patterns of global migration.

The net result of the nationalist impulse in history – plus the move toward greater precision – was, very simply, that there were few major advances in world history writing, much less teaching, during the nineteenth or early twentieth centuries. There was real irony here, because in the actual world, contacts among societies were accelerating during precisely this period: but very little historical work reflected these wider developments. To be sure, it was interesting that a German scholar in the 1880s produced an encyclopedia of world history (later translated into English in the United States, with more recent editions still available). This showed a recognition of some possible relationship between historical information and the world linkages taking shape. But the *Encyclopedia* filled mainly with coverage of European history, with only passing references to other major societies and virtually no material at all on places like Africa until the Europeans started intervening.

It was only toward the middle of the twentieth century that a few ambitious historians began to turn to the project of sketching a global, rather than national or at most regional, framework for the human experience. Arnold Toynbee, a British historian, began his monumental *Study of History* in 1934; it focused particularly on exploring the rise and fall of empires – the case of the Roman Empire was the clearest prototype, but Toynbee was deeply interested in India, and his approach certainly could be extended to world history more generally. A more decisive set of developments took shape by the 1960s. Several prominent American historians, headed by William McNeill, began actively advocating world history and writing books, both texts and works aimed at a more general reading public, illustrating what world history could cover. These studies understandably replicated aspects of the Western civ approach, in looking at the formation of great cultural and political traditions, but they now embraced China, India and the Middle East as well as the Mediterranean and the West. At the same time, a surge in area studies programs began to produce new knowledge about key regions such as Africa or the Middle East.

A second source of new inspiration came from several key universities in the communist world. Marxist ideology had always set forth a global vision, though it long focused on the emergence of Western capitalism. By the 1960s, Marxist scholarship was advancing enough that other societies, again particularly in Asia, could be encompassed. The University of Leipzig, in the German Democratic Republic (East Germany) thus set up a comparative history curriculum in the 1960s, with new centers for studies on Africa, Asia and Latin America. This advanced in 1974 toward a more global approach, under the umbrella of the comparative study of revolutions in modern times. This framework would lead directly to Leipzig's leadership in world history initiatives in contemporary Germany, even as the explicitly Marxist approach has receded after the end of the Cold War.

None of this, however, yet produced a world history movement. Pioneers like McNeill provided approaches and inspiration that would ultimately create a larger, younger generation of world history scholars – but in an immediate sense, nothing much seemed to happen. McNeill pushed for a world history program at his home base, the University of Chicago, but he simply could not dislodge a well-established and deeply popular Western civilization course. Most European countries, particularly outside the communist bloc, continued to emphasize national histories without much modification, whatever leading historical scholars were doing. Many new nations, for example in Africa, if they had opportunities to do much in the history field, either persisted in teaching European history (a heritage from the colonial past) or more understandably tried to emphasize a national approach. The communist regime in China, though linked to more global Marxist scholarship, in fact installed a national history emphasis, highlighting the Chinese experience through the lens of Marxist analysis. Finally, the rise of area studies work, though again immensely important for the future, in a way distracted attention from world history itself. Scholars grew so excited about the separate contours of East Asian, or Middle Eastern, or Latin American history that they either ignored or actively resisted any impulse to dilute their new-found discoveries by paying much attention to developments at the global level.

Global engagements by the 1960s, in other words, encouraged attention to historical experiences outside the West, but this had little impact on actual teaching programs (aside from the new availability of a category interestingly called "non-Western" civilization courses, at various universities) and did not generate more than a trickle of attention to world history per se.

It was only in the 1980s that world history began to come into its own. In the United States, world history courses began to emerge at scattered four-year colleges and a few community colleges. A number of high school teachers began moving in the same direction, often by adding some African or Asia coverage to the European history course. There was a point at which teachers at various levels were trying to come to terms with the fact that they had growing numbers of African American, Asian American and (soon) Latino students in their classes, and that some of these students were also more aware than their predecessors had been of their own proud cultural traditions. These teachers needed to find historical materials with which these students could identify, and the best among them also wanted to use the opportunity greater diversity suggested to provide educational gains for students of all origins. It was also unavoidably clear by the 1980s that the framework within which the United States operated – as a Cold War leader, as an active international business engine, as an exporter and importer of culture – was no longer primarily bounded by interactions with Europe. A new history course was essential to help prepare students to operate within this framework, as citizens, as workers, even as informed tourists. As in the 1960s, but now much more decisively, world history as a field was emerging partly as a result of the efforts of particular teachers and scholars, but also in a real sense as a product of a changing real-world environment. And while the movement took its most coherent shape initially in the United States – where a new World History Association formed in 1982 as a collaboration among innovative teachers at the college and high school levels – the same pressures would soon encourage new exploration and educational programs in other countries.

Once launched, sustained by growing interest as well as the broader factors underlying the need for world history, the movement has so far proved unstoppable, despite nationalist concerns and despite the U.S. Senate slap in 1994. The University of Hawaii introduced the first explicit Ph.D. field in world history in 1986. A new *Journal of World History* followed in 1990. An ambitious Advanced Placement course in world history opened in 2001, and with 21,000 initial test takers proved the largest new program in the history of the whole Advanced Placement program; it also showed the most rapid expansion, with well over 100,000 test takers within a mere five years. In the United States, and in several other societies, world history was moving from the status of precocious upstart to a measurable maturity, producing courses and programs at various levels and increasingly inspiring innovative research.

FEASIBILITY

World history has a clear set of purposes, and its recent history shows how these purposes have emerged in relation to changing international relations and a changing student mix. But there's a final set of introductory issues, reflecting the newness of the field but going beyond, that also must be faced: is the enterprise feasible? World history, after all, potentially covers everything. And historians – as students all too clearly grasp – tend to be fact rats, treasuring the accumulation of data and tending to believe always that more is better than less. Simply look at the standard world history textbook in the United States: 1100–1200 pages, crammed with material. There is, to be sure, a welcome move to shorten this average a bit, but the amassing of material cannot be denied. It was revealing, back in 1994, that when the American group produced its statement of world history standards it offered a neat 300-page outline, with almost 50 major topic headings – in contrast to geographers, who, when assigned a similar task of developing teaching and learning goals in their field, managed a tidy 65-page pamphlet.

All this said, the first lesson for anyone venturing into world history teaching and research is stark: DARE TO OMIT. Even the 1200-page textbook has omitted countless possible data points and has done clear injustice to at least some major societies in the world (example: in most world history texts in the United States, southeast Asia receives far less attention than its importance and complexity arguably deserve).

The problem, in a field that loves to uncover facts about the past, is defining *what* to omit. Ask world historians what topics are indispensable in the field, what any educated student should know, and the list will almost certainly be intimidating – particularly if there is more than one world historian in the room. Each significant religious tradition, each major change in trade patterns, each stage in technological change, key national patterns within larger regions like Western Europe, possibly all the leading Chinese dynasties, the succession of leading empires in the Middle East – the shopping list is huge. And it's hard to deny that world historians, in their passion for coverage and detail, risk dropping the ball when it comes to manageability. One of the reasons for a statement of the Basics in the field – for this book, in short – is to offer a clearer means of making sure that the global woods are not lost amid the world history trees.

Yet there are several approaches that do provide standards of selection, that do set forth larger organizing principles that highlight an achievable number of topics and provide standards for what data can be excluded from a meaningful program. We'll be exploring several of these in the chapters that follow, but a preview is appropriate.

First, no world historian believes that one must proceed century by century; all world history programs emphasize larger time periods that have some definable basic themes. Within each period, exploration of more complex evolutions remains possible, depending on the space available, but the conceptual key is the larger chronological pattern. In this schema, world historians argue that fundamental changes in world history really don't occur all that often; world history *time*, as a result, is more manageable than one might expect.

Second, no world historian pretends to explore every definable region or (in modern times) nation – remember that right now there are over 200 United Nations members, and several other states that would like to add to the list. All world historians deal with larger regional patterns and interactions. Again, more detailed exploration can work within this framework, as time permits. The larger regional generalizations, however, allow world historians to make space more geographically manageable than one might expect (though there is more debate and anguish over this than there is about the world history units of time).

Third, no world historian pretends that all conceivable historical topics must figure in the world history canvass. Several projects have attempted to offer a subject focus to help guide manageability: the Advanced Placement course thus offers five headings: humans and the environment (embracing categories like demography, disease, technology); development and interaction of cultures (religion, science, art and so on); state building and conflict (types of governments, empires and nations, revolutions); economic systems (agriculture, trade, the industrial revolution and so on); and finally the development and transformation of social structures (gender, family, race, social and economic class). This is still a long list, but it stimulates some selectivity.

There's another angle to manageability: all world history programs reflect some combination of three basic approaches. Understanding these approaches, and the fact that their number is limited, undoubtedly advances the feasibility goal.

First: most, though not all, programs work on defining major societies or civilizations, tracing their evolution and interaction, and using active comparison to help make sure that world history does not spin off into separate and unrelated strands. We will see that this first approach makes some world historians a bit nervous, for several reasons, but it is also very difficult to avoid entirely. Comparison is the crucial analytical glue that holds this approach together.

Second: increasingly, world historians are deeply interested in contacts among major societies, and what results when contact occurs. How do societies learn from each other, force adjustments from each other, or seek to regulate interactions? Comparison helps in this approach too – when two societies interact, it's important to compare what each brings to the table. But analysis here expands beyond comparison, to embrace skills appropriate to understanding interactions and also, over time, how patterns of interaction change.

Third: even beyond contact, world historians are interested in identifying and tracing larger forces that impinge on a number of different societies, even when they're not in direct contact. These forces can include patterns of migration, contagious diseases, diffusion of technologies, missionary cultures, and trade and more recently environmental impacts. World history allows a comparison of how different societies react to these common forces, thus linking the third approach to the first; it encourages an effort to explore how contact relates to the larger forces. Again, change in the configuration of larger forces is – along with shifts in patterns of contact – one of the things to look for in organizing and defining world history time periods.

Tracing and comparing major societies; looking at the evolution and results of contacts; tracing reactions to larger forces, but also changes in their nature – this is a manageable list of organizing principles. It underpins world historians' abilities to manage time and geography (and to some extent topics). It helps to define what kinds of materials can be discarded – for example, detailed internal developments in individual nations.

World history is an ambitious subject. For many, it's exciting for precisely this reason. It's undeniably challenging, even for enthusiasts. But it is in fact manageable. It does not have to be – it must not be – simply a race to memorize as many data points as possible. Even granting historians' problems with saying no to data, it offers principles of selection.

TWO FINAL (SMALL) PRELIMINARIES

World history normally uses BCE and CE (Before the Common Era, and Common Era) rather than the conventional, Christian-derived BC (Before Christ) and AD (Anno Domini, or in the year of our Lord). The time periods designated are the same (in contrast to the traditional Chinese, or Jewish, or Arab calendars). But the different labeling is designed to make the whole thing somewhat less ethnocentric and culture-specific, since world history is about the whole world and not just one religious experience, however undeniably important. This all might seem pretty harmless and even trivial, but it is vital to note that some people find the change in nomenclature very upsetting, because of its implications about the centrality of Christ's birth. Historians who use the world history dates publicly may be accused (as the author has been) of atheism, intolerance and other evils. Again, world history can be a touchy subject.

Second preliminary: we are in this book using the term world history, rather than global history, but both are often in play. World history is the more common current label. Global history often means the same thing. For some, however, there is an implication in global history of more intense focus on contacts and interconnections, though as we have seen these emphases must be embraced in world history. For certain critics, worried about globalization and eager to protect the national tradition, "global" may be a more inflammatory term than "world." Finally, as we will discuss later on, there is an interesting group that uses the term "new global history" as distinct from world history: the new global history argues that a fundamental transformation in the human experience took place in modern times – most probably the second half of the twentieth century – that should be the focus of historical inquiry. They believe that world history wrongly downplays the watershed in favor of more extensive and even-handed coverage of earlier developments and transitions. This approach deserves consideration as one of the issue sets that must be confronted even in the larger, more conventional framework of world history.

THE MAIN POINTS

Most world historians believe that their subject, though oddly recent as a major educational category, is a vital component of any good history curriculum and an essential building block in programs of international or global education. The subject flows from the work of many eminent scholars and teaching practitioners, but also from our changing times, reflecting new diversities and new or enhanced global connections. The field embraces important debates, challenges and uncertainties but it has defined a core manageability that lies at the heart of more detailed inquiries. Launching world history inevitably generates controversy, but it also generates rapid and extensive interest from a variety of quarters. The field's core purpose – using a new kind of history to explore the origins and evolution of current global relationships and issues – ultimately defines both the feasibility of the teaching program and its obvious attraction for people who seek a better understanding of the global relationships that surround any nation today.

FURTHER READING

Patrick Manning's *Navigating World History* (New York: Palgrave Macmillan, 2003) is the best single introduction to the field, with useful references.

The Journal of World History is also an excellent source for diverse recent work on world history, from authors in various regions. *Teaching World History in the Twenty-First Century: A Resource Book,* edited by Heidi Roupp (Armonk, NY: M.E. Sharpe, 2010) also contains compelling, recent essays on the subject. The American Historical Association publishes many good works on the subject, among them Jerry Bentley's *Shapes of World History in Twentieth Century Scholarship* (Washington, D.C., 1996) that provides articles on global and comparative history that are useful.

Reliable internet resources include the American Historical Association (AHA) which serves the broad field of history (www.historians.org); and the World History Association (www.thewha.org), a leading learned society for the promotion of world history teaching and scholarship. See also *World History Matters,* http://chnm.gmu.edu/world-history-matters/, which is hosted by George Mason University; and *World History Connected,* http://worldhistoryconnected.press.illinois.edu/, which is an affiliate of the World History Association.

2

A WORLD HISTORY SKELETON

This chapter is an introductory guide to world history, a summary of a standard framework – a textbook in a few pages. Emphases are threefold: first, most obviously, since history is a time-based discipline, what are the definitions of key time periods and what are the main features of each? Second, within each period (different regions move into different positions depending on timeframe) what are the geographical highlights? And third (some periods feature change in certain topics – providing the main focus – but substantial continuities in others) what are the key subjects in each period? The chapter introduces the more analytical focus explored in later chapters, but it can also be used as a highlights-in-advance approach to any of the large textbooks that will expand on each of the points here in greater detail. It's the woods, for this purpose, in advance of the trees.

THE EARLY STAGES: 2.5 MILLION BCE TO 10,000 BCE

All comprehensive world histories start well before what historians used to call the advent of recorded history, i.e. the arrival of writing. The early human story is also enlivened by all sorts of recent new discoveries, based on fossil finds in Africa and on improved methods of carbon testing for dates and also genetic analysis. From the advent of human-like species to the timing of human migration from Asia to North America, novel findings have pushed back what had been regarded as standard dates and opened some exciting debates about the long period of early human history and about the relationship of human evolution to that of other primates.

For world history purposes, several points are central. First, the human species went through complex and lengthy evolutionary development, from its first appearance two and half million years ago, or perhaps even longer, in East Africa. Various distinct species not only emerged but in some cases migrated to other areas. The arrival of the species to which all contemporary people belong, *Homo sapiens sapiens*, was a late result of this long process. Gradually, through superior adaptability – particularly for changing conditions in hunting animals, where short bursts of speed became a priority; through outright warfare; and through intermarriage, *Homo sapiens sapiens* became the only human species around, upwards of 120,000 years ago. Crucial genetic changes, including the capacity for speech and language, accompanied this final (to date) major evolutionary process.

TECHNOLOGY AND MIGRATION

Early humans also generated at least two other basic achievements. First, as humans operated within a hunting-and-gathering economy, where men hunted and women gathered nuts, seeds and berries, they gradually became increasingly skillful tool-users. Humans are not the only species to find objects in nature that they can use as tools and weapons, but they ultimately gained the ability not only to find but to manufacture tools, shaping bone, wood and stone to serve more precise purposes, particularly for hunting and fishing (including ultimately manufacturing early boats). The advent of the Neolithic, or new Stone Age period about 11,000 years ago, capped this process of tool improvement within the confines of stone-age technology.

The second big news was migration, which several human species had accomplished but which *Homo sapiens sapiens* took up about 70,000 years ago. The reasons for migration were simple: hunting and gathering groups, usually about 70–80 strong, need a lot of space, on average over 2 square miles per person. Any small population increase forces some members of the group to push out into new territory, or there will not be enough food. Most important was the surge of groups from Africa across the Red Sea to the Middle East, from which some bands headed north and west, into the Middle East, Central Asia and Europe, and another stream ultimately reached eastern Asia. From Asia also, groups ultimately ventured to the islands of Southeast Asia and to Australia – at a point at which the Southeast Asian land mass extended much farther southward than is the case today. And, by 25,000 BCE or perhaps earlier (there is debate about this), other Asian groups crossed from Siberia across what was then a land link to present-day Alaska, from which some moved quickly southward, reaching other parts of both North and South America. By 10,000 BCE a small global human population – about 10 million people in all – inhabited virtually all the areas where people now live. This dispersion reflects the adaptability of the human species. It also produced increasing differentiation, though not at the basic genetic level (which means, the different groups of humans could still interbreed) but rather in languages and cultural practices.

In sum: for the long early periods of human history, look for: the main phases of the evolutionary process but particularly the ultimate characteristics of *Homo sapiens sapiens*; grasp the nature and the social implications of the hunting and gathering economy; look for the major phases of tool use and particularly the improvements attained by the time of the Neolithic period. And, perhaps above all, register on the nature, timing and implications of human migration.

MAIN PERIODS IN WORLD HISTORY: ONE SKETCH

ADVENT OF AGRICULTURE

The early periods of human history were transformed by the arrival of agriculture, or what is sometimes called the Neolithic Revolution. This is the first sweeping change in the basic context for human history, and world historians usually pay a great deal of attention to it. Responding to improved tool use and, probably, reductions in the big game available for hunting, people (surely inspired by imaginative women, who had been the seed-handlers

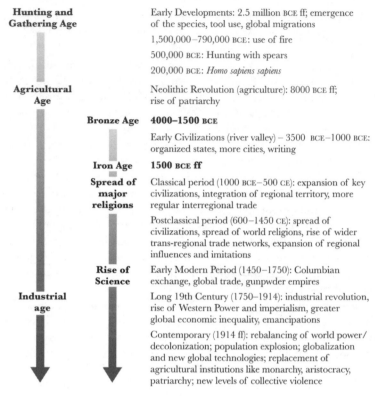

Hunting and Gathering Age		Early Developments: 2.5 million BCE ff; emergence of the species, tool use, global migrations
		1,500,000–790,000 BCE: use of fire
		500,000 BCE: Hunting with spears
		200,000 BCE: *Homo sapiens sapiens*
Agricultural Age		Neolithic Revolution (agriculture): 8000 BCE ff; rise of patriarchy
	Bronze Age	**4000–1500 BCE**
		Early Civilizations (river valley) – 3500 BCE–1000 BCE: organized states, more cities, writing
	Iron Age	**1500 BCE ff**
	Spread of major religions	Classical period (1000 BCE–500 CE): expansion of key civilizations, integration of regional territory, more regular interregional trade
		Postclassical period (600–1450 CE): spread of civilizations, spread of world religions, rise of wider trans-regional trade networks, expansion of regional influences and imitations
	Rise of Science	Early Modern Period (1450–1750): Columbian exchange, global trade, gunpwder empires
Industrial age		Long 19th Century (1750–1914): industrial revolution, rise of Western Power and imperialism, greater global economic inequality, emancipations
		Contemporary (1914 ff): rebalancing of world power/ decolonization; population explosion; globalization and new global technologies; replacement of agricultural institutions like monarchy, aristocracy, patriarchy; new levels of collective violence

Figure 2.1

for the species) began deliberately planting grains. They also domesticated a wider range of animals (the dog had been the first domestication achievement, of obvious assistance in hunting), including cows, horses, sheep and pigs.

The advent of agriculture is both historically tricky, and fundamentally important. The tricky aspects are, first, that agriculture did not arise tidily in all areas at the same time. Furthermore, some regions only adopted agriculture quite recently, long relying on different economic systems which, while less significant than agriculture, also deserve attention. Finally, even when agriculture was established and began to spread, the process of dissemination was surprisingly slow.

DATES AND DISSEMINATION

The first instance of agriculture emerged in the Black Sea region in the northern Middle East, around 9000–8000 BCE, and was based on the cultivation of barley, oats and wheat. From this site, agriculture would gradually spread to other parts of the Middle East, to India, to northern Africa (and possibly all of Africa) and to Europe. But agriculture was separately invented in at least two other places: Southeast Asia, based on rice cultivation, around 7000 BCE; and Central America, based on corn, around 5000 BCE, with dissemination from both of these centers. There may have been other separate inventions, for example in sub-Saharan Africa. We don't know for sure in some cases if the arrival of agriculture reflects dissemination or new discovery.

Even when agriculture was established, it spread only gradually. It took thousands of years for agriculture to reach key parts of Europe, for example. The slowness of diffusion had two causes. First, contacts among peoples were halting, particularly outside individual regions: news of major developments did not travel fast. But second, there were lots of reasons not to appreciate agriculture. Compared to hunting and gathering agriculture required more hours of work (particularly from men); it challenged male hunting prowess; it led to other problems, such as a new incidence of epidemic diseases once groups of people began to settle and concentrate rather than moving around. It was, in sum, a big change, and many groups long resisted even when they knew of the possibility. It is historically and philosophically important to realize that agriculture was not pure gain but, like most major shifts in human history, an interesting mixture of plusses and minuses.

Finally, partly because of climate and soil conditions, a number of regions did not adopt agriculture at all until much more recent times. Huge areas, including much of North America, persisted in hunting and gathering, though this was sometimes spiced by a bit of seasonal agriculture. Other major human groups moved to a nomadic herding economy, rather than agriculture, relying on domesticated animals (horses, cattle, camels) rather than farming. Nomadic groups never developed the population levels of successful agricultural regions. But their control over key regions and their ability to contact agricultural centers through trade, migration and invasion give them great importance in world history until at least 500 years ago. The most important nomadic region was central Asia, but nomadic tribesmen in the Middle East and parts of sub-Saharan Africa also deserve attention; the key herding regions developed in and around a great arid zone that stretches from the Sahara desert in the West to central Asia and western China in the east.

The Neolithic revolution, then, involves a somewhat scattered chronology, a surprisingly slow and uneven spread, and the emergence of important alternatives.

It was, nevertheless, a fundamental development in world history. Even with its drawbacks, like greater vulnerability to contagious disease, it produced larger food supplies than hunting and gathering could, and so permitted expansions in the human population. Agriculture allowed families to have more children and, even with characteristically high infant death rates, more children surviving to adulthood. Its service in expanding the human species was ultimately irresistible to many regions. Human population began to grow, doubling every 1600 years to reach a level, worldwide, of 120 million by 1000 BCE.

NATURE OF AGRICULTURAL SOCIETIES

This means in turn that, several thousand years ago depending on region, a new economic system took shape that would last until about 300 years ago (and that still predominates in many places). It's vital to realize that most of textbook world history coverage involves agricultural societies, usually with a fairly short section on the experience of the human species before agriculture and a longer section on industrial, or post-agricultural, changes. World historians can easily demonstrate that within the framework of agriculture, important changes and important variations would occur. Some agricultural societies, for example, never generated many significant cities, whereas others produced a lively urban economy and culture. So there is every reason to devote substantial attention to the ways different agricultural regions changed and diverged. But still, the fact that they were agricultural commands attention.

For agricultural societies shared several key characteristics, no matter where they cropped up and no matter how much they changed. Most agricultural societies quickly developed more permanent settlements, usually in peasant villages. This allowed communities to clear land; dig wells; and sometimes set up irrigation systems; but also to develop connections that only a settled existence could allow. All agricultural societies focused primary attention on growing food; most generated a bit of surplus, but it was limited. Few agricultural societies could ever free up more than about 20% of the population for nonagricultural pursuits, including urban life, and many kept even more on the land. Limited surplus also helps explain why so many agricultural societies generated a well-defined, but rather small, elite of wealth and power. Agricultural societies also emphasized marked disparities between men and women, in patriarchal systems that gave men preeminent power. Historians have discussed why this occurred, in contrast to hunting and gathering societies where women's economic importance assured them a more prominent role and voice. Because agricultural societies increased the birth rate, more of women's time was taken up in pregnancy and early child care. In most (though not all) cases, men took primary responsibility for bringing in the major crops, assisted by children and, in peak season, by their wives. Women's day-to-day work was also vital, in caring for gardens and animals around the house, but men overmatched them and presumably claimed disproportion power in consequence. Additionally, agriculture redefined childhood, seeing children primarily as a source of family labor. This explains why an increase in birth rate was vital, but also explains why agricultural societies emphasized the importance of obedience and discipline as primary qualities for children.

A final note: all agricultural societies generated some concept of a week (though they differed widely on how many days it had), the only major time unit that is invented entirely by humans, with no relationship to any natural process. Presumably weeks were desirable to provide a leisure day, amid intense work, and to permit time for some trading activities. Often, a period for spiritual activity was designated as part of the weekly cycle, instead of simply leisure time per se.

Despite a common foundation, agricultural societies varied greatly, even in the specific interpretation of features like patriarchalism. But the common features and constraints must be factored in for any comparison, for there were limits to variation as well.

CIVILIZATION

Several thousand years after the arrival of agriculture, some human societies began to change and, in many ways, complicate their organizational structure. The result – the more complex structure – is what many world historians mean when they talk about the advent of civilization. Compared to other kinds of agricultural societies, civilizations had more surplus production, beyond what was needed for subsistence. They could on this basis afford more occupational specialties, from government personnel to skilled craftspeople. They also, typically, displayed more inequality than non-civilizations did. Beyond this, civilizations normally had more elaborate cities, and a clearer urban culture, than non-civilizations did, where if there were cities at all they were usually small and scattered. More cities also meant more need for trade, to provide food and the exchanges necessary for food. Civilizations had formal governments and at least small bureaucracies, rather than the less formal leadership present in simpler societies. They were societies with states, rather than "stateless". Most civilizations, finally, had writing, which helped government bureaucracies; which helped trade, through better and more standard record-keeping; and which encouraged fuller retention of knowledge than purely oral transmission could.

LOCATIONS

The first civilization emerged in the Tigris-Euphrates river valley – the region often called Mesopotamia – around 3500 BCE. It was preceded by some important technological improvements with the agricultural economy, including the wheel, the use of metal (bronze, an alloy of copper and tin) for tools and weapons, and of course the invention of the first writing system. The Sumerian people introduced their cuneiform writing style, and then the first known organized government on the heels of these key developments. Early civilizations emerged in several other centers soon thereafter: in Egypt; in the Indus river valley of present-day Pakistan; and, a bit later, in northern China along the Yellow River. All four of these early civilizations operated around complex irrigation systems along major rivers. Irrigation required particularly elaborate organization and legal arrangements, lest one group take all the water and deprive everyone else; this undoubtedly encouraged the need for more formal government. Irrigation also helped generate particularly productive agriculture, which provided further resources that could be used to help support cities and generate tax revenues for governments. A fifth early civilization case, considerably later, emerged in Central America with the Olmec peoples, but this was not based on irrigation systems primarily.

It is important to note that, for a long time, many agricultural peoples did not generate civilizations. They operated successfully without the civilization apparatus, often with some small cities as trading centers but without writing or formal government. Civilization did tend to spread, partly through conquest, but in some places, like West Africa, "stateless" agricultural economies continued to function until relatively recent centuries. Civilization, in other words, was not a quick or inevitable product of the advent of agriculture.

RIVER VALLEY CIVILIZATIONS

In North Africa and in several parts of Asia, the four early civilization centers operated for many centuries. They developed more formal legal structures; the first known law code, the code of the King Hammurabi, came from a later Mesopotamian regime. The centers developed characteristic monuments, the most famous of which emerged in Egypt with the great pyramids. They produced art and literature, some of which has survived to the present. The first known literary work, almost certainly a written record of what had been an oral story, the *Gilgamesh*, came from Mesopotamia. Some of them generated extensive trade and travel. From Mesopotamia, for example, traders sought sources of tin and also precious material, like the stone *lapis lazuli* found only in Afghanistan.

For world history, the most important achievement of the river valley civilizations was to generate types of social infrastructure that would not have to be reinvented, including writing and formal laws. Early civilizations introduced money, obviously vital for more extensive trade. Several of them invented further technological improvements, for example in the manufacture of pottery. Several also developed new understandings in mathematics and science, revolving around issues of measurement and calculation of the seasons. So: look at the early civilizations to determine what their durable achievements were, that might outlast their own centuries of operation. Urban development, for example, was one common feature: there were about eight cities in the world with over 30,000 inhabitants by 2250 BCE, but sixteen cities that large by 1250 BCE.

At the same time, each of the river valley civilizations had something of its own character, and together they allow the possibility of comparison. It is also true that we know far more about some of the river valley cases than others – the Indus river valley's history is particularly challenging, because scholars have not yet translated the writing system. Egypt and Mesopotamia are most commonly compared, with different religions and cultures, different political systems and social structures, even (though both were patriarchal) different approaches to women.

Comparison of internal characteristics leads to two other topics for the early civilization period: the durability of characteristics and regional outreach. We know that the river valley civilizations introduced specific arrangements from which we continue to benefit – like the Mesopotamian notion of measuring in units of 60, which we still use for calculations of the circumference of circles or minutes in an hour. Did they also generate more profound cultural features that still shape particular societies? Some scholars have argued, for example, that Mesopotamia and Egypt developed ideas about the separation of humans from nature that would later shape major religions like Christianity and Islam, and that also differ from characteristic south or east Asian approaches to the same subject. The fact is that we don't know enough about either early comparisons or later connections to be sure.

We are on firmer ground in noting how the river valley civilizations generated influences that went beyond their initial centers, helping to spread particular civilization systems. Egypt, for example, had trade and cultural influences both on other parts of the eastern Mediterranean, including Greece, and even more important on the upper Nile river valley, where they helped shape important African societies like Kush and, later, Ethiopia. Equally clearly, a series of aggressive Mesopotamian empires gained control over larger parts of the Middle East, bringing a variety of active contacts as a result. It was not surprising, thus, that a Mesopotamian story about a great flood showed up later in Jewish culture and the Bible. The Indus

River civilization traded widely. All of this set the stage for later contacts and expansions.

END OF THE EARLY CIVILIZATION PERIOD

The early, or river-valley, civilization period drew to a close around 1000 BCE, though there were no sweeping events to mark the change. The period of big empires ended for a time in the Middle East. This allowed some important smaller societies to emerge, particularly in the eastern Mediterranean. The sea-faring Phoenician peoples were one such, forming cities at various points around the Mediterranean Sea. Of even more lasting importance were the Jewish people, whose first definite historical records date from about 1100 BCE and who began to shape the world's first great monotheistic religion, of importance in its own right and the seedbed of two other later, great religions from that region of the world. Egyptian dynasties continued for a time after 1000 BCE but with declining vitality. The Indus River civilization disappeared entirely – and we don't know exactly why, possibly because of local environmental exhaustion. China, the last of the river valley civilizations, demonstrated greater continuity, with the Zhou dynasty, formed shortly before 1000, continuing, though amid weak organization, for several centuries beyond.

What is clear, particularly outside of China, is that a new series of civilizations, partly co-located with where the early civilizations had been and certainly building on their achievements, was actively in the wings by 1000 BCE or shortly thereafter. These civilizations would assume greater power than the river valley societies had mustered. They would also benefit immensely from the use of iron, rather than bronze, for tools and weapons. Iron use, introduced in southwestern Asia around 1500 BCE, generated a metal far stronger than bronze, the basis both for greater agricultural productivity and for fiercer warfare. Here was a technological underpinning for the next great era in world history.

THE CLASSICAL PERIOD, 1000 BCE TO 600 CE

The most obvious focus of world history during the 1500 or so years after 1000 BCE is on the expansion and development of major societies in China, India, Persia and the Mediterranean. In each of these cases, some combination of government conquests (facilitated by tighter military organization and iron weaponry), new migrations of people, and diffusion of key cultures led to the establishment of civilization zones much larger than what the river valley societies had attained. China thus expanded to embrace more southern territory. Indian culture and social organization fanned out from a new base along the Ganges River, gradually reaching additional portions of the subcontinent. A new Persian Empire arose and for several centuries controlled the Middle East and some territory beyond. Finally, beginning with expansionist Greek city states and ending with the vast Roman Empire, a Mediterranean civilization developed that would ultimately embrace southern Europe, substantial chunks of the Middle East, and North Africa.

These expanded territories had to be linked and integrated in various ways. Governments began to promote new road systems, a vital aspect of developments in China, Persia and Rome. The Persian Empire even established the world's first postal service, along with carefully-spaced inns for travelers. All the classical civilizations worked to promote internal trade, taking advantage of specialty areas within the society. Thus China built north-south canals to facilitate exchanges between rice-growing regions in the south and grain growing areas in the north. Greece and Rome promoted active trade in the Mediterranean, with olives and grapes coming from southern Europe in exchange for grains from places like North Africa. Cultural integration involved efforts to spread belief systems and even languages to provide more common currency within the expanded territory. Thus the Chinese promoted the use of Mandarin for the upper class throughout the country, while in the eastern Mediterranean use of Greek spread well beyond Greece itself. In India, the development of the Hindu religion, but also the spread of Buddhism provided common religious interests through much of the subcontinent. Greek and Roman artistic styles spread widely through the Mediterranean region, establishing monuments that still draw tourists today from Turkey to Tunisia to France and Spain. Finally, all of the expanding civilizations at various points established empires, uniting all or (in India's case) most of the civilization territory under a single government. The establishment of the Chinese Empire, particularly under the Han dynasty, was the most important imperial development, in terms of long-term consequences, but Persia, Rome and the two imperial periods in India (Mauryan and Gupta dynasties) were milestones as well. Many empires tried to solidify their political hold by moving peoples to promote further loyalty and integration: the Chinese moved northern Chinese populations south, to further unity, while both Greek and Roman governments sent out colonies to help tie some of the more distant regions to the homeland.

The classical period is defined, then, above all by expanding large-regional civilizations, with new forms of economic, cultural and political integration creating new ties within the new regional units.

DISTINCTIVE FEATURES

In the process, each of the new civilizations also established a sense of core traditions, which in many cases would outlast the classical period itself. These traditions were cultural above all, but they also included political impulses and social ideas. Each civilization thus developed some defining characteristics that provided at least some degree of unity within the territory – though more clearly among upper than among lower classes – and that could differentiate each major civilization from the other. Civilization here takes on a second meaning: not only a form of human organization, but also a set of identities and identifying features.

Not surprisingly, given this definitional aspect, each set of markers was somewhat distinctive. The Indian tradition was defined by a strong religious impulse, with Hinduism ultimately the most important carrier and with artistic achievements illustrating religious beliefs; but also by the beliefs and practices surrounding the caste system. Political achievements were significant but less central. China, in contrast, came to emphasize the importance of a strong state and a bureaucratic upper class, linked to the importance of Confucian philosophy and social beliefs. The classical Mediterranean tradition, amplified in different though related ways by Greece and then Rome, emphasized the importance of politics and (most commonly) aristocratic rule, but also the characteristic literary and artistic traditions that related to a civic, polytheistic religion. The Mediterranean also was defined by substantial reliance on slavery, a labor system that was much less important in India and China.

The Persian case is a bit harder to handle. The powerful Persian Empire was matched, on the cultural side, by the development of the distinctive Zoroastrian religion. Persia would be conquered however by Alexander the Great, coming from Greece, and Persian and Greek elements intermingled for a time. Later, after the classical period, Persian culture would be transformed by the arrival of Islam. Still, a Persian tradition (for example, in art) and a separate Persian Empire periodically revived. The contemporary nation of Iran builds on this complex tradition.

Overall, however, the classical period gains significance in world history from the fact that each key regional civilization established a number of lasting features, including central cultural traditions, important elements of which can still be identified today. The classical achievements continue to inspire awe: contemporary Iranians for example cast back to Persia as part of their own sense of identity, just as many Westerners or Russians remain fascinated with Greece and Rome. In key cases, classical traditions continue not just to impress, but to shape ongoing reactions. India grapples with legacies of the caste system, though it was outlawed in 1947. China continues to reflect particular interests in the importance of a strong state and political order. In no case does the classical tradition define contemporary civilizations, for far too much has changed; but the influence is real.

The significance and durability of classical traditions, but also key differences, obviously suggest the importance of comparison in approaching the classical period as a whole. The Roman and Han Chinese Empires form a particularly obvious comparative pairing, but other opportunities are also vital, for societies in general and for individual topics like religion or science. The similarities among the classical experiences must be retained as well as the different features and identities.

COMPLEXITIES IN THE CLASSICAL PERIOD

The formation of extensive regions and some durable traditions constitutes the most obvious structure for the classical period and for comparison, but there are other issues to watch as well:

- First, the classical systems did not emerge fully formed; in each case, they developed over time. Classical China, for example, developed a strong state tradition only after several centuries.
- Second, the classical traditions must not be oversimplified. Each of these large, complex civilizations embraced a variety of currents. Indian religion and religious art deserve note, obviously, but so does the rise of Indian science and mathematics. And there were several major Indian religions at this point.
- Third, analysis of the separate classical civilizations must not prevent identifying some underlying dynamics. For example, the use of iron plus the political and economic innovations in the classical period encouraged population growth. Between 1000 BCE and 1 CE world population doubled, to 250 million people. This was a global development to an extent, reflecting the expansion of agriculture, but it concentrated particularly in the classical civilizations. At their height Rome and China each had populations of about 55 million people.
- Fourth, attention to the separate patterns of the classical civilizations must be balanced by awareness of their interactions, and their related impact on some surrounding regions. Patterns here varied. Greece and Persia, and later Rome and Persia, had many contacts, particularly through war. Exchanges between India and China heated up toward the end of the classical period with the main result the importation of Buddhism in China. More important still were the two major sets of routes that linked the classical civilizations and also drew in other participants, for example with Ethiopia in northwestern Africa. A series of overland connections, from western China through central Asia and into India, Persia and through the Persian road network to the Mediterranean, have been called the "Silk Roads." Interest in Chinese silk spread among the upper classes even as far away as Rome. Most of this trade was through short, several-hundred-miles stages. At most one Roman group went directly to China, and mutual Chinese–Roman knowledge was limited. The trade route, however, did create awareness of the desirability of products from distant points. A second network ran through the Indian Ocean. Romans were sending expeditions to India on a regular basis by the time of the Empire, from ports on the Red Sea,

and groups of Romans actually set up export operations in Indian cities with particular interest in pepper.

DECLINE AND FALL

Between 200 and 600 CE the great classical empires fell. The Han dynasty in China was first to go, collapsing in 220 and opening a 350-year period of frequent invasions and small, warring states. The Roman Empire began to decline from about 180 onward, gradually losing territory and suffering less effective government. The imperial government in the West collapsed entirely in the fifth century. A separate Roman government had by that point been set up in Constantinople (formerly Byzantium), and an eastern or Byzantine Empire, focused on present-day Turkey and southeastern Europe, persisted for several centuries. India's Gupta Empire collapsed in the sixth century, after a period of decline.

The end of the classical period reflected important invasions by hunting and gathering or nomadic peoples. Particularly important were incursions from the Huns of central Asia. Different Hun groups attacked China, a bit later Europe, and also the Guptas. A devastating series of epidemic diseases hit the classical world, particularly China and Rome, disrupting the economy and morale alike. New political problems also jeopardized trade, including the Silk Roads, generating new economic constraints on individuals and governments alike.

The accumulation of changes added up to the end of the classical period. For many regions, political and economic stability deteriorated for some time. Political unity in the Mediterranean world ended outright, and has never since recovered. Change in India was less drastic. Though large political units became less common, unless imposed from outside, Indian economic and cultural life continued along familiar patterns. Hinduism and the caste system spread southward in the subcontinent. In China, a long period of disruption yielded, late in the sixth century, to a new dynasty and the revival both of imperial government/bureaucracy and of Confucianism. The different regional results of the period of classical decline were extremely important in shaping the next period in world history. They also affected ongoing use of the classical heritage, which was much more direct in China, India and Byzantium than around the bulk of the Mediterranean.

THE POST CLASSICAL PERIOD, 500 CE TO 1450 CE

This period is variously named, and is sometimes subdivided. World historians largely agree, however, on several major themes for the centuries involved – themes to which most major societies had to react. The onset of the period was shaped by the turmoil in much of the classical world. Several regions, including Western Europe and India, did not recover the degree of political organization they had developed during the classical period.

During this period, a large number of new regions established the apparatus of civilization, including more important cities and formal government. Japan, Russia, northwestern Europe, additional parts of sub-Saharan Africa (both West Africa and eastern Africa down the Indian Ocean coast), additional sections of central and Andean America were key cases in point.

During the period also, a number of newer areas, in trade contact with more established centers, began a process of deliberate imitation, particularly in technology and culture. Japan thus explicitly copied many features from China, Russia looked to the Byzantine Empire, Western Europe borrowed both from Islamic civilization and from Byzantium, Africa interacted with Islam and so on. Imitations often involved religion or philosophy, artistic forms, as well as agricultural techniques.

The two most important overarching themes in the postclassical period were the spread of major missionary religions and the acceleration of trans-regional trade among societies in Asia, Africa and Europe. Both of these developments permanently altered the framework for world history and the experiences of literally millions of people in different areas.

MISSIONARY RELIGIONS

Buddhism was a well established religion by 500 CE. Christianity had started five centuries before, gaining ground slowly within the Roman Empire (about 10% of the Roman population was Christian by the fourth century), then much more rapidly when the Roman government began to provide support. Islam, the newest world religion, began around 600 CE and would initially enjoy the most rapid spread of all. All three of the expanding religions reflected the political and economic troubles of the late classical period, which prompted more interest in otherworldly goals. They were also strongly supported by vigorous missionary efforts. During the post-classical centuries, hundreds of thousands of people converted, usually from some form of polytheism, to one of the world religions, one of the great cultural shifts in human history.

TRADE CONNECTIONS

The second great change involved intensification of trans-regional trade, backed by important improvements in ships and navigational devices. Arab traders, soon supplemented by Persians and others, established a strong route across the Indian Ocean, linking the Middle East to India, Southeast Asia and the Pacific coast of China. Clusters of Arab traders located in southern Chinese ports. Connecting to this route in turn was an Arab–African network down the African east coast; a trans-Sahara overland connection from West to North Africa; a route from Scandinavia through western Russia to Constantinople, with contacts with Arab trade; a bit more gradually, links from Western Europe to the Mediterranean and hence to Arab merchants, Japan's regular trade with Korea and China was a final major connection. More regions, exchanging more goods of wider variety, were important components of this whole network. Other interactions were attached: Arabs, for example, learned the Hindu numbering system and then spread it more widely, with the result that Europeans called the numbers Arabic as they began to adopt them. Knowledge of paper, a Chinese invention, spread more widely. Maps and travel accounts both expanded and improved.

Technological advances included new sailing ship design, by the Arabs, and toward the end of the period additional shipping improvements from China. The introduction of the compass, initially from China, was a huge navigational gain, and it spread quickly around the Indian Ocean and thence to Europe.

Contacts facilitated technological exchanges and exchanges of different crops (new strains of wheat, for instance, spread from Africa to Europe) that helped improve agriculture. This in turn began to accelerate world population gains following the declines in the late classical period, with levels reaching almost half a billion by

1350 CE. At the end of the period, the rapid spread of bubonic plague from China through the Middle East and Europe briefly reduced population levels, however.

The postclassical period began to draw to a close when Arab power and political effectiveness started to decline, by the twelfth to thirteenth centuries. New commercial rivals for the Arabs arose, including European (particularly Italian) merchants in the Mediterranean but also Indian and Southeast Asian Muslims in the Indian Ocean. The Arab empire – the caliphate – began to lose significant territories, and it was finally toppled late in the thirteenth century.

THE MONGOLS

Briefly, a new force arose to help organize the trans-regional framework. Mongol conquerors from central Asia swept over China, into the eastern part of the Middle East, and conquered Russia. Interlocking states, or khanates, provided new travel security from Europe to Asia, and the Mongols proved tolerant of new contacts. Land-based trade and travel increased, and so did exchanges from Asia westward. Europeans learned, mainly from China, about printing, explosive powder, playing cards and other items. The Mongol period also rearranged relationships, reducing for a time Russia's regional role; Japan, unconquered despite two Mongol invasion attempts, rethought its relationship with China which, having yielded to the Mongols, now seemed less lofty. African regions, not directly involved in the Mongol exchanges, did not acquire the technologies that Europe gained.

Mongols were expelled from China at the end of the fourteenth century, and China briefly launched a massive series of trade and tribute expeditions through the Indian Ocean as far as Africa. A policy change ended these expeditions in 1439. By the middle of the fifteenth century, with Chinese trade becoming less venturesome, European expeditions down the African coast began to suggest a more assertive European commercial role. At this time also, a new Turkish-led Empire, the Ottomans, formed in the Middle East, and would conquer the Byzantine Empire after 1453. Russia, at the same time, began creating an independent zone around Moscow, pushing the Mongols back. This accumulation of changes – capped by the European discovery of the Americas in 1492, clearly brought the post-classical period to an end. Trans-regional trade would soon be replaced by global trade, under a new level of European influence. The spread of world religions did not cease but, except in the Americas, became a more minor theme as most of the religious map of Asia and Europe was fairly firmly set.

THE EARLY MODERN PERIOD, 1450 CE TO 1800 CE

Three major changes define this period:

GLOBAL EXCHANGE

The Americas began to be included in global interactions for the first time, and then after the middle of the eighteenth century the same applied to Australia and key Pacific island groups. The first implication of these inclusions was a biological exchange (often called the Columbian exchange), between the previously isolated territories and the rest of the world. New diseases reached the Americas (and later the Pacific) from Europeans and Africans, including measles and smallpox, which decimated the population. This opened the way, in the Americas, for the importation of new peoples, from Europe but even more, through the slave trade, from Africa to supply necessary labor. Columbian exchange also brought animals from the old world to the new, where previously the range of available domesticated animals had been surprisingly sparse. Columbian exchange also brought new world foods into use elsewhere, including corn, the potato, chili peppers and other crops. The ultimate impact of these new foods helped fuel a new acceleration of population growth, from about 375 million in 1400 (after the plagues) to almost a billion in 1800 (Chinese population alone soared to 350 million). This global change occurred despite rapid population decline in the Americas until recovery began after 1700.

GLOBAL TRADE

The second major development was the formation of a truly global economy, with European merchants and commercial companies serving disproportionately as carriers. Other societies continued to use Indian Ocean routes, but Europeans took over almost half of these, mainly through the use of force. Europeans monopolized trans-Atlantic and trans-Pacific exchange. Crucial for the Europeans was the ability to use silver mined in the Americas for the purchase of Asian goods, including both manufactured products (the word china came into European languages in the seventeenth century) and spices and other products like tea and coffee. Europeans also profited hugely from the Atlantic slave trade, though within Africa itself this was largely organized by African merchants and rulers. The economic relationships in much of the global economy became markedly unequal, with Europeans gaining large profits and dependent areas like Latin America relying on the export of cheap goods generated by servile labor. Strong elements of this unequal pattern persist to the present day.

The global economy had other players, however, notably in Asia. While the Atlantic economy was clearly Western-dominated, the world economy was not, though the West gained a growing role. Chinese production and export of silks, ceramics and other goods won it the largest amount of American silver in exchange, and India (with printed cotton cloth and spices) came in second. The Middle Eastern economy, though no longer in prime place, remained important. New levels of commercial and manufacturing activity defined early modern Asia in important ways.

It's also been argued – though hard to prove – that labor changed in this global economy. Thanks to the new levels of Atlantic slavery plus more pressure for commercial production in Europe, the Americas and Asia, plus the burdens of population growth, the intensity of human labor may have increased in the early modern centuries, from more use of children to more need to continue working hard in later age.

EMPIRES

The third big global development involved the formation of a number of new empires. This reflected growing political capacity in many regions, as well as the importance of new military technologies – notably cannon – and new attention to military training and organization. "Gunpowder" empires formed of course under

European sponsorship – Portugal and Spain, followed by Britain, France and the Netherlands set up massive overseas empires in the Americas and in ports and island groups in parts of Africa and Asia. But new land-based empires also emerged. Russia was not content to chase the Mongols back to central Asia, but began to expand further in central Asia, in Europe and in East Asia, becoming a significant player in Eurasian affairs. In the process, the separate importance of central Asian nomads, such a major factor in world history through the Mongols, dropped away. The Ottoman Empire in the western Middle East was rivaled by a Persian Safavid Empire farther east. In India, the new Mughal Empire (like the Ottomans and Safavids, Muslim-ruled) gained substantial territory on the subcontinent. These new empires brought significant changes to the regions involved, and some of them had lasting impact into the twentieth century and, in Russia's case, beyond. Along with the revived Chinese empire and the European holdings, most of Asia and the Americas came under imperial sway.

Biological exchange, with important population and migration results; the new world economy, with its complex relationships; and the new age of empire and new levels of military activity – these were the key themes of the early modern period. They draw attention to the growing vigor of Western Europe, but also to Russia, the Asian empires, and the new interactions among Europeans, Native Americans and imported African slaves that would gradually forge a new society in Latin America.

SCIENCE

A final major development began to take shape in the early modern period, but its global significance was not immediately apparent. On the whole, global cultural exchanges were limited in these centuries, as if societies reacted to new trade contacts and empires with an implicit desire to keep identities separate. Japan, indeed, deliberately adopted a policy of substantial isolation in part because of fear of too much Christian influence from Europe.

In Western Europe, however, particularly from the seventeenth century onward, a real scientific revolution occurred that would have huge implications for world cultures and technologies over time. Triggered by major discoveries on planetary motion, gravity and the circulation of blood, scientists began demonstrating that major advances in knowledge were possible, beyond anything traditional learning had to offer, through the application of scientific methods. Their achievements began to push science, rather than religion or philosophy, to the forefront of intellectual life, with implications for technological change, education and even the study of human society (key social sciences, like economics, began as a result to emerge in the eighteenth century). This upheaval, with consequences but also bitter debates still reverberating today, was initially a largely European enterprise. By the eighteenth century, however, Western science began to interest people in places like Britain's North American colonies and Russia, and by the nineteenth century American and Russian scientists would become full participants in the larger scientific endeavor. Japanese leaders, informed by contacts with the Dutch about European advances, began to allow translations of European scientific and medical works, and a bit of interest developed in the Ottoman Empire. This was not yet, by 1800, a clearly global current, but it would become one, which adds to the areas in which the early modern period was a seedbed for significant and durable world-historical changes.

THE LONG NINETEENTH CENTURY

Most world histories carve out a relatively short period of time, beginning (with no particular single event) in the late eighteenth century, ending with World War I (1914–18). Calling this the long nineteenth century at least provides a suitable label.

The key development in these decades, and what marks them off from the early modern period, was the advent of the industrial revolution, initially in Western Europe and the new United States. The core of the industrial revolution, in turn, was the application of fossil fuels – at first, through the deployment of a usable steam engine, from the 1770s onward – to manufacturing and other activities. The use of new energy sources, along with better manufacturing equipment and the growing use of factory organization for work, allowed a massive increase in production. The industrial revolution changed the human economy and society as much as the advent of agriculture had done, though the implications took some time to work out and in fact are in process still today.

Application of new technology to agriculture, along with other changes, spurred on food production. More people could now commit to urban life. Britain became the world's first half-urban society in 1850 (the world as a whole became half urban only in 2006). Overall population levels increased rapidly, doubling during the nineteenth century to 1.75 billion people. Improved public health measures, based in part on new understanding of disease contagion and spreading particularly in the second half of the century, helped push population levels up as well.

Application of new technology to transportation and communication yielded the telegraph, railroad and steamship during the first half of the nineteenth century, greatly reducing the time needed to communicate and transport around the world. This facilitated new levels of migration, with millions of people pouring out from Europe but also now from Asia, to the Americas and Australia above all. World trade soared, and the construction of major canals (Suez and then Panama) further supported this upsurge. Here was the technological basis for a first phase of globalization.

The long nineteenth century was, however, only an initial stage in the industrial revolution as a global phenomenon. It had consequences virtually everywhere, but the period was marked by the fact that outright industrialization was monopolized by Western Europe and the United States until the very end of the nineteenth century, when Japan and Russia began to join the parade.

INEQUALITIES IN POWER

Near-monopoly, in turn, had several key consequences. The first was military. Using new technologies and the industrial production of weapons − rifles, light cannon, and then the machine gun − Western forces became better armed than competitors anywhere in the world, and small numbers of Western troops proved capable of defeating sometimes thousands of more traditionally-armed opponents. The long nineteenth century was dotted with demonstrations of the West's global military superiority. Egypt was briefly conquered in 1798; China was defeated in the first Opium War of 1839, and forced to open its markets; an American fleet threatened Japan in 1853 and began a process of rapid change and international openness there. No society could now remain separate from a Western-dominated world orbit.

Second, following on the military, came a burst of Western imperialism. Mainly during the second half of the nineteenth century, European powers took over virtually the whole of Africa, and also gained new colonies in Southeast Asia and the Pacific.

Finally, the West's industrial dominance created massive new regional inequalities. Western factory output undermined traditional manufacturing in many places, which then turned to imports of goods like textiles. At the same time Western demand for foods and raw materials spurred more production of goods that relied on cheap labor. Latin American dependence cheap exports of minerals, sugar, coffee and similar products increased. Africa was converted increasingly to similar low-cost production.

REVOLUTIONARY IDEAS

Industrialization and new Western power shaped the long nineteenth century, but there were some other themes and complexities. Late in the eighteenth century the West generated a series of political and sometimes social revolutions. These revolutions, headed by the American rising in the 1770s and then the great French Revolution of 1789, challenged the rule of kings and the power of aristocrats. They tossed up new ideas about personal freedom, constitutional and parliamentary rule, and also nationalism. Some movement toward democratic structures was involved as well. The revolutionary era continued through risings in several European countries in 1848. It included a major cluster of wars for national independence in Latin America, mainly between 1810–20, that threw off Spanish rule in most of the region and created a series of independent republics. (New Latin American nations often suffered from political instability because of internal unrest, lack of experienced leadership, and economic problems, the first example of "new nations" problems that would surface more widely in the twentieth century.)

The fires of revolution were not yet global. For much of the world, new imperialist controls and economic exploitation were far more direct than any talk of freedom, democracy and nationhood. The new ideas did spread, however. Nationalism encouraged independence movements against the Ottoman Empire, particularly in the Balkans. Indian nationalists began organizing for greater voice in the 1880s, and later would turn to a goal of national independence. A new, reform-minded Turkish nationalism developed within the fading Ottoman Empire. Japan and several other countries copied the idea of constitution and parliament, though with carefully restricted powers under the control of ministers appointed by the emperor.

Revolutionary ideas found other targets as well. Efforts to promote new rights for women gained ground, producing formal feminist movements, mainly in the West but with some global outreach, by the late nineteenth century.

EMANCIPATIONS

New sentiments also roused against slavery and the slave trade and against the harshest forms of serfdom. The European revolutions abolished serfdom outright by 1849. Abolitionist movements, centered in the West, moved against the slave trade even earlier. Britain largely ended the Atlantic trade in 1808. Several American states and new Latin American nations abolished slavery early in the nineteenth century as well. And the movement spread, spurred by new humanitarian ideals and also by a belief that modern conditions demanded more efficient and mobile labor than slavery could provide. Russia abolished serfdom in 1861; the United States proclaimed slave emancipation in 1863. Brazil and Cuba ended slavery a bit later, while European imperialists abolished the practice at least of literal slavery in Africa. These changes were facilitated by massive population growth, that allowed slaves to be replaced by relatively cheap labor fueled by the new levels of immigration.

FIRST WORLD WAR

The long nineteenth century ended with World War I. This was the bloodiest war ever fought to that point, with millions killed and millions more wounded. Here was an opening to what turned out to be a very violent twentieth century. The war generated unprecedented government controls over the economies, labor force and propaganda in key countries, setting the basis for new government forms, like communism, fascism and Nazism, later on. It spurred a revolution that shook the Russian empire, and it led directly to the collapse of the Ottoman Empire and also to the creation of a whole series of small new nations in east central Europe. While military activity concentrated in various parts of Europe, offshoot battles not only in the Middle East but in the Pacific prompted change, including Japanese hopes for additional empire. Quite widely, the war encouraged global nationalism: nationalist goals stood tall in the war itself and were proclaimed (though not fully observed) as the basis for war settlement, and participation of colonial troops from India and Africa in the war spread ideas of nationalism more widely in these regions. Above all, the war deeply weakened the European powers, and while the results were not immediately apparent, this was the beginning of the end for the kind of military and political dominance Western Europe had exercised during the long nineteenth century. A globally-imbalanced period was drawing to a close.

THE CONTEMPORARY ERA IN WORLD HISTORY

There are two built-in difficulties to defining the contemporary period in world history. First, we're still in it, which means that we don't know how the story ends with regard to many crucial themes. We know what the themes are – for example, a literally global effort to find political alternatives to monarchy and empire – but we don't know how they will be resolved. This is an inherent contrast with all previous periods.

Second, the last hundred years have seen all sorts of developments and much messiness. There were the decades dominated by world wars and depression, then decades partly framed by the Cold War, then the end of the Cold War. Some world historians reduce this problem by taking the smaller chunks of time rather than an overall and still-ongoing period. This solution however may bog us down in too much detail.

The issue is: what's the big picture, in terms of themes that capture the most important directions in world history over the past century, without any set assumption about when this period will end?

CHALLENGES TO THE WEST

First – and this is where World War I comes in as launching the new period – power relationships have been rebalanced, against earlier Western predominance. Nationalist challenges to Western rule and then the surge of decolonization after World War II reduced one of the West's classic holds over many parts of the world. Efforts like enhanced guerilla warfare and the rise of military arsenals in newly-independent nations did not eliminate Western military advantage, with the United States included, but progressively limited it after World War II. The economic rise of Japan to the number two spot in the world, and then the surge of economies in China, India, Brazil and elsewhere toward the end of the twentieth century made it clear that the economic dominance of the West was also under review. There were many paths toward a greater share of wealth on the global economy, including control over vital oil resources, but expansion of industry or related services was the most important route: industrialization began to spread more widely. The West remains an extremely important factor in world affairs, with great political, economic and particularly cultural influence, but its relative place has declined. In 2008, in response to major financial crisis, the United States assembled key powers to discuss response, but instead of calling on the leading Western nations plus Japan and Russia (the "group of eight" that had met often to oversee world economic affairs), it was clear that there must now be a "group of twenty," more fully to represent Asia, Latin America and other regions. The power alignment had clearly changed, and the process clearly continued into the twenty-first century.

POPULATION EXPLOSION

Theme two must be the unprecedented expansion of human population, tripling in the space of 100 years to a total of over 6 billion worldwide. Regional involvements varied. By the early twentieth century Western society had experienced what is called the *demographic transition*, with low birth rates and also low infant death rates and expansion of longevity. Other societies entered this transition later on – Japan, for example, by the 1950s, key parts of

Latin America by the 1970s. But many regions maintained higher birth rates, yielding massive population growth and high percentages of young people in India, the Middle East, Africa and Latin America. Overall, global population growth also supported vast waves of migration, from poorer to wealthier regions, particularly after World War II. Migration from Africa, Latin America, parts of the Middle East, south Asia and the Philippines was particularly impressive, with destinations in the industrialized regions and generating unusual amounts of cultural intermixing and, sometimes, tensions. Massive population growth also strained environmental resources, contributing to new global issues in this arena.

GLOBAL TECHNOLOGY

The contemporary period in world history is also defined – theme three – by a recurrent round of basic innovations in global communication and transportation and, after World War II, an intensification of globalization overall. The advent of overseas radio and air travel, in the 1920s and 1930s, followed by commercial jets after World War II (and the identification of "jet lag" in 1963), followed by satellite communication for telephones and television, followed around 1990 by the effective introduction of the civilian Internet – all added up to unprecedented speed and volume for moving people, goods and information around the world. This was matched at the policy level, after World War II, by new institutions like the International Monetary Fund and what ultimately became the World Bank, aimed at facilitating trade and minimizing international economic crises. International agencies like the World Health Organization provided new levels of global political contact, along with new non-governmental organizations like Amnesty International, bent on global campaigns over human rights and other issues. National policy decisions were added in: China in 1978 moved toward unprecedented links with the rest of the world in trade but also education and culture, and Russian policy reorientation in 1985 worked in the same direction. Over time, in other words, the institutions and impacts of globalization, from a clear technological foundation, had increasing influence in virtually every region of the world – even when the result included new resistance or even outright protest.

SOCIAL AND POLITICAL UPHEAVAL

The final (fourth) set of new themes was more amorphous, but powerful in its own right: over the past century, most societies in the world moved to supplant some of the most characteristic systems of the agricultural past. This was not a globally-organized movement. It involved massive revolutions in some societies, headed by Russia and China. It embraced key aspects of national liberation movements as well. Political and social structures changed clearly. Where operative monarchies or imperial regimes had existed in 1914, they were largely replaced by new kinds of authoritarianism or by democracy by the twenty-first century. The dominant landlord class was increasingly supplanted by a new upper middle class (including government and party bureaucrats in some societies but revolving particularly around big business). Major revolutions attacked the aristocracy directly, and economic changes that reduced the importance of agriculture did the rest. Massive social change even extended to gender relationships, at least to some degree. More educational and political opportunities for women, developing almost everywhere, challenged and arguably displaced traditional patriarchy. Regions varied, to be sure. Viable monarchies remained in a few Middle Eastern and North African countries. Women's rights were more bitterly contested in some places than in others. Urban locations changed more rapidly than rural – but urban settings were increasingly becoming the global norm. Cultural systems, also, changed less systematically: the rise of science, consumer values, and political ideologies like nationalism and communism challenged older beliefs, but religion not only persisted but developed new vigor in many regions from the 1970s onward. The pattern of change, overall, was definite but complicated.

The basic themes of the contemporary era: shifts in global power relationships, population explosion and environmental challenge, globalization itself, and a pattern of basic political and social change provided a framework for a host of specific regional reactions and events.

CONCLUSION

Periodization is vital to world history, helping to identify big changes to which many societies had to respond. Arguably the greatest shifts involved the agricultural and industrial revolutions, but the spread of the world religions, with their implications not just for cultural but also political and economic life, deserves attention as a significant marker, and so do changes in contact patterns like the inclusion of the Americas.

FURTHER READING

A good overview is Edmund Burke III, David Christian, and Ross Dunn, *World History: A Compact History of Humankind for Teachers and Students: the Big Eras* (Los Angeles: National Center for History in the Schools, 2009). See also Jared Diamond's *Guns, Germs and Steel: the Fates of Human Societies* (New York: W.W. Norton & Company, 1999); and *First Civilizations: Ancient Mesopotamia and Ancient Egypt* by Robert Chadwick (London: Equinox Publishing, 2005).

For specific periods in history, see Richard L. Smith's *Premodern Trade in World History* (New York: Routledge, 2009); *Rome and China: Comparative Perspectives on Ancient World Empire,* edited by Walter Scheidel (New York: Oxford University Press, 2009); Toby E. Huff's *The Rise of Early Modern Science: Islam, China and the West* (Cambridge, UK: Cambridge University Press, 2003); Alexander Chubarov's *The Fragile Empire: A History of Imperial Russia* (New York: Continuum, 2001); and Edward L. Dreyer's *Zheng He: China and the Oceans in the Early Ming Dynasty, 1405–1433* (New York: Longman, 2006). See also Peter N. Stearns' *The Industrial Revolution in World History,* 3/e (Boulder, CO: Westview Press, 2007). For the contemporary period, several texts provide good overviews on specific, current topics, including *Turbulent Passage: A Global History of the Twentieth Century,* 3/e, by Michael Adas, Peter N. Stearns and Stuart Schwartz (New York: Longman, 2005).

3

HABITS OF MIND IN
WORLD HISTORY

By now it should be clear that world historians have a vigorous commitment to making as sure as possible that many people know some vital facts about the global past. An educated public should know something about the emergence and impact of the key religions; they should understand the implications of the move to an agricultural and then an industrial economy. They should grasp major phases in the patterns of contact among different regions and, in more modern times, the development of outright global institutions and patterns. And the list could go on considerably. Being an educated person in today's world, and having the information needed to operate effectively in that world, requires some specific knowledge.

World history, however, is more than fact lists. Indeed, even the facts won't help much if they can't be rearranged, combined and used in active analysis. So world historians, along with other historians and educators, have been working with increasing focus on what kinds of habits of mind should be developed within and as a result of a world history program. Students need to be aware of identifying and illustrating these skills and habits in order to make the most out of a world history program at any level.

Different compilations inevitably generate different lists of skill sets, but in fact there are no huge disputes and some of the variation is largely a matter of labeling. Overall, it's best to think of world historical mental habits in three categories: first, and quickly, some basic goals in which world history students participate along, hopefully, with students in lots of other courses in many disciplines. Second, some thinking skills that attach to historical analysis in general. One eminent educator has argued that thinking historically is an "unnatural act," but whether that's true or not it is obviously the case that many students don't come to a program with innate abilities to think as historians do and it is also (if less obviously) the case that their overall analytical capacities will improve if they do learn to think that way. And finally, third, there are two or three habits of mind that specifically attach to world history, and these warrant separate and explicit attention.

BASIC SKILL SETS

Students in world history programs gain opportunities to expand certain basic skills – but it's also vital wherever possible not to focus so intently on the fundamentals that there's inadequate time for more advanced analytical components. Good world history programs expect some writing and ideally some oral presentations as well. Students can anticipate expectations ranging from appropriate grammar and word choice, to logical organization to (ideally) a certain level of stylistic felicity. The key challenge is for students to become accustomed to using world history facts and data to form arguments. There's often a certain tension here. Because world history programs do involve a certain amount of factual coverage, and because there's a need or desire to make sure that students do the reading and don't fall too far behind, some testing will place a premium on memorization. Students will be asked to identify key features of Confucianism or the industrial revolution – just to be sure they are competent in some of the empirical building blocks of world history. But this kind of testing should not distract from the greater goals, of developing the capacity to use knowledge of Confucianism to answer larger questions about the distinctive nature of Chinese society or the ways in which Chinese social systems in practice actually fit Confucian guidelines. Always, the intent is to combine factual accuracy with an ability to marshal empirical evidence to answer questions that go beyond regurgitation.

There is always a danger in textbook-based history courses – and world history is no exception – that diligent students will mistake careful memorization for the kind of analytical agility they need in using facts to answer questions. (Instructors sometimes call this impulse, admittedly inelegantly, a data dump.) A student encounters a writing assignment, for example, that asks for assessment of changes and continuities in Russia's position in the world economy in the eighteenth and nineteenth centuries and says, aha, it's about Russia, and proceeds to list every feature of Russia, from Peter the Great to World War I, that can be remembered – wars, cultural Westernization, serfdom, political conservatism and all – regardless of actual relevance. The real task is more complicated: knowing the data is essential, but selecting from it and recombining it to deal with the question asked is equally essential.

Effective argument (whether written or oral) thus involves stating a clear analytical problem, rather than just jumping in with some summaries of factual data. It requires some kind of logical sequence in an argument, in which the answer to the problem is presented but with an orderly citation of evidence as proof. Where time and sophistication permit, noting the most plausible objections to the solution to the problem, or at least additional issues that must be resolved, will actually enhance credibility. Forming arguments, and knowing the presentation and selection techniques that convey arguments, must be central to the process of doing world history well.

HISTORY SKILLS AND HABITS

History as a discipline involves several analytical categories. A key building block centers on handling source materials and also dealing with debated interpretations. History is not unique in defining opportunities here, but history sources, in particular, because they derive from different time periods, raise some particular challenges that win wide attention, and students can approach these challenges explicitly. A second category involves using historical data to test larger theories or propositions about human behavior or historical patterns, and also claimed relationships between developments at one time and those at another – the kind of thinking wrapped up in historical analogies. World history courses, which typically work hard on handling sources, are less focused on the skills associated with theory testing, but some awareness is appropriate.

The grandmother of all historical habits, however, involves dealing with change over time. Here, a number of steps can be identified that break this category into sequential chunks. Specific world history emphases, within the larger change-over-time rubric, can also be highlighted in advance.

INTERPRETATION AND SOURCES

Diverse interpretations are a standard part of work in history (and many other disciplines) – historians love to disagree with each other, sometimes almost to excess. The category has not, however, been a clear component of world history until relatively recently. World historians worked hard to get their field established. Often, they spent a fair amount of time expressing themselves through textbooks, and textbooks tend to emphasize (or overemphasize) certainties rather than deliberately raise debate. As world history matures, different interpretations begin to emerge more clearly. And imaginative teachers often believe that precisely because textbooks often loom large, it is vital to get students thinking about alternative viewpoints, often treating textbooks themselves in terms of points of view rather than definitive statements of truth.

We'll be talking later, in Chapter 9, about some of the leading current controversies in the field. For now, the point to establish is that students in world history should expect to gain experience in identifying the fact of controversy and figuring out how to manage the problems that controversy presents. They should be able to articulate what a significant debate is about and how the positions of protagonists can be explained, what kinds of evidence are used by each "side," and, ideally, how the debate might be resolved – through some sort of compromise, or through additional evidence. They should be able to incorporate the controversy into their own argument about a world history issue, and though they cannot be expected to resolve the controversy they can be asked to indicate what line of argument strikes them as most reasonable and accurate, and why.

An example is essential to pin down these general points. The issue is: what impacts did the Cold War have on world history between the late 1940s and the late 1980s? As part of exploring the issue, students encounter a basic debate about what caused the Cold War in the first place. One line of argument holds that the Cold War originated from the aggressive intentions of the Soviet

Union, bent on expanding its territory, and the related global ambitions of communist ideology, which hoped and expected to export a socialist system around the world. Against this, both Soviet apologists and revisionist Western scholars emphasize how cautious the Soviet Union was, how it was principally eager to control a buffer zone around its own territory to prevent a repetition of something like the Nazi invasion, and how American policy, though ostensibly responding to the Soviets, actually frightened the Russians while encouraging a variety of global interventions from the United States side. A student should be able to define what the debate is all about and explain what kinds of evidence each party to the controversy uses; the student should be able to speculate, at least, about what other factors might explain the positions involved. American revisionists, for example, began to surface in the 1960s, as the Vietnam War dragged on – timing here may help explain why they began to differ from earlier American Cold War analysts. Differences between American and Soviet scholarly context also enter in, as well as ideological positions (communist or leftwing vs. conservative and capitalist). A student may also be able to explain why one position seems better-founded than the other. And the student should certainly be able to situate the controversy in the larger assignment of figuring what Cold War impacts have been – an assignment that includes but goes well beyond the responsibility issue. None of this requires the student to resolve the controversy – after all, scholars who devote their lives to the field continue to argue, and students have far less time, data or experience at their command. But understanding and interpreting the debate can be expected, as part of making students more comfortable with the fact that historical interpretations are not cut and dried, that they compel a capacity to grapple with division and uncertainty.

After all, in dealing with real-world issues today, debates are plentiful. Experience in world history should encourage students to step back from, say, a media blitz about a current international issue to offer a definition of the debate (rather than a thoughtless embrace of simply one side), a weighing of the evidence and the reasons for differing points of view, and a determination of what steps would provide the most responsible resolution – through compromise, additional data or even further points of view. Passionate commitment may usefully result, but it should come after, not before, a recognition of standard controversy management. Experience in world history actively contributes to this vital but challenging process.

Use and interpretation of sources is a far more familiar aspect of world history programs than is exposure to conflicting viewpoints. There's nothing more popular with history teachers who are eager to escape an exclusive textbook diet than to add some primary materials to the mix, and world history has participated in this trend extensively. Students in good programs, from high school onward, can expect to encounter expectations that they improve their skills in assessing documents and in marshalling them to form arguments. They want to be able to use and combine documents to respond to questions that go beyond simply summarizing the material itself. For many teachers, the skills involved are fundamental to the capacity to "think like a historian," and indeed it is true that historical scholars must learn how to interpret a variety of materials as the basis for their own accounts. Perhaps more relevant – though there's nothing wrong with thinking like a historian – is the fact that people are presented with primary materials all the time, whether it's politicians' speeches or advertisements – and the capacity to interpret them, to assess bias and meaning, is fundamental to functioning adequately in modern life. Gaining experience and improving skills here, as with handling diverse interpretations, provides services well beyond the world history classroom.

USING SOURCES

Historical source materials come from all sorts of settings. The one thing they have in common: they were not written with twenty-first century readers in mind, so of course they require different kinds of reading, and more active interpretation, than textbooks or other contemporary accounts demand.

Sources encourage speculation and further questions, which promote better understanding of a past society even when definite answers require further information. It is vital to know what the sources do NOT reveal, and to think about what other kinds of data would be useful. To take an obvious example: written sources are much more likely to uncover patterns in the upper classes than those of the lower classes.

Several brief samples provide specific illustrations about challenges and opportunities in reading and interpreting primary sources (quoted passages are from documents directly):

One of the earliest written sources available is the Babylonian emperor Hammurabi's law code (Mesopotamia, around 1700 BCE). The code was not written to tell modern-day students about Mesopotamian social structure, but it's fairly easy to read it to discover that there were at least three social classes, because there were three levels of fines for harming someone, depending on whether they were slaves, ordinary people or free men (the elites). It's easy also to identify the society as patriarchal, for women had far fewer rights than men.

Other passages are less straightforward. For example: "If a man charges a man with sorcery, and cannot prove it, he who is charged with sorcery shall go to the river, into the river he shall throw himself, and if the river overcomes him his accuser shall take over the man's house. If the river shall show the man innocent because he comes forth unharmed, he who charged him with sorcery shall be put to death. He who threw himself in the river shall take over the house of his accuser."

What is this passage all about? What problems is it trying to deal with, and how do modern societies deal with the same problems? Does the passage reveal aspects of Mesopotamian religious beliefs? About property structure? Why did Mesopotamians believe that a river would demonstrate guilt or innocence? These questions can be answered, at least in part, from the passage, but obviously they require some thought. The reader can even answer the question: did Mesopotamian schools offer swimming lessons?

It is also possible to speculate about what the practices described in the passage mean. Think of the river-dousing in terms of problem-solving. What problem was Mesopotamian society trying to deal with in the stipulations about what would happen if the accused emerged safely from the river. How does a modern society try to deal with the same problems – for we've abandoned the river technique? Why would Mesopotamia (and many other pre-modern societies) have chosen the different approach: what different beliefs are involved, what are the differences in the professionals available to help the justice system?

For additional data: how often were people accused of sorcery? Did Mesopotamians believe in monotheism? These are fine questions, but they cannot begin to be answered from this passage.

Ban Zhao (c. 44–117 CE) was an upper class woman in Han China who wrote a widely read and often republished manual on women's roles and conduct. A girl should be put below the parents' bed to show that she was lowly and weak and should concentrate on humbling herself before others do. "Girls should also early learn to be diligent in household work. ... Yet only to teach men not to teach women, is this not ignoring the essential relations between them? It is the rule to begin teaching children to read at the age of eight, and by the age of fifteen they ought to be ready for cultural instruction. Only should girls' education as well as boys' not follow this principle?" As Yin and Yang are not of the same nature, so man and woman have different characteristics. Men are honored for strength. A woman is beautiful on account of her gentleness.

What's the main point of this passage? What issues require some extra interpretation? Why is this document significant evidence for world history (or why not)?

Some questions can be easily answered from this passage: did the classical Chinese believe that men and women were equal? What kinds of personal qualities did Ban Zhao think a good woman should have?

Reasonable speculation can lead toward further answers: is this a document applying to the upper classes or to Chinese society as a whole? How could Ban Zhao use beliefs about unequal roles to argue for certain rights for women? Does a document of this sort suggest that some individual women could generate significant achievements in classical China? Did even those who advocated education for some women believe it should be the same as that offered to boys? Were women likely to be as violent as men in classical China? Did Ban Zhao believe that gender relations were properly organized in the society around her, and if not what might be a concern?

Good questions but ones that can't be answered from this passage: how widespread were educational opportunities for women in classical China? Did upper-class women have more children than lower class women? Did upper class men take more than one wife? How did women's education in classical China compare to that in classical India? Did lower-class women in China ever have access to schooling? Dealing with these important questions requires thinking about other kinds of desirable evidence.

We also know that the skills involved are not easily acquired. This is why a leading student of history learning, Sam Wineburg, has argued that mastering documents from the past is an "unnatural act." He shows that experienced historians, with no particular content knowledge of, say, American history, are much better than very bright high school students who've had a year of explicit study in understanding how to handle American historical sources. It's hard to read documents in light of past rather than present language and values, which is where the experience comes in.

World history arguably poses additional challenges, because one is dealing not only with sources from the past but with materials from quite different cultural traditions, multiplying opportunities for misunderstanding and oversimplification. The challenge obviously has a flip side: gaining greater mastery represents a huge step forward in understanding how other societies work, precisely the kind of understanding that can serve in dealing with global materials even outside the classroom.

World history students can actively practice steps like recognizing reasons for bias or point of view in documents, seeking the specific historical context in which a source was generated, putting different kinds of sources together to form an argument, even in recognizing what sources do NOT say – in identifying areas where additional documentation would ideally be required for any definitive historical statement. They can also expect to use different kinds of sources. Materials from subordinate groups, like women and peasants, gain growing importance in world history precisely because they allow access to vantage points outside official rhetoric. Artistic materials and cartoons enter the picture, offering their own challenges of interpretation but providing vital additions to available evidence. Perhaps a bit more haltingly, statistical materials, like census records or production and trade figures, also factor in, sometimes providing vistas on ordinary life – on family structure, for example – that more qualitative evidence ignores or downplays.

World history courses may pay some attention to helping students assess two common uses of history, well beyond the handling of sources, though this is not usually front and center on the habits of mind agenda.

First: some scholars, whether trained historians or not, have at various times projected certain kinds of laws, or unvarying basic models, describing the human experience over time. Professional historians usually shy away from this type of intellectual activity, as inevitably slighting the complexity and variety of the past, but proposals do crop up from time to time. The approach invites evidence-based testing. In the world history field probably the most challenging overall model, though somewhat out of favor today, involves the idea that major societies inevitably or at least normally go through a standard life cycle. Arnold Toynbee's work sketched a process whereby successful societies pass through a period like infancy, when they form their identities and begin a process of growth; then a long experience of maturity, marked by fuller articulation of characteristic ideas and institutions and successful functions; but then a period of ageing and decline. Toynbee's model drew particularly on the pattern of the Roman Empire (in the western Mediterranean primarily), but there were references to many other examples, and certainly the profile might seem in general to be a plausible one. Most world historians would probably object to the model based on the greater diversity of experiences they can cite (how, for example, could the model apply to the Chinese experience since the classical period? Here is a society that displays ups and downs but has never "fallen," in the manner of the western Roman Empire.) But the main point is the use of historical thinking and data to evaluate generalizations of this sort, to provide critical perspectives and tests. And while the Toynbee model has gone out of fashion, more recent (and admittedly more modest) work by scholars like Yale University's Paul Kennedy sets up generalizations that can be tested and that again invite both use and evaluation through world history analysis. Kennedy talks about types of societies that overextend their territorial conquests and ultimately undermine their success through this excess of ambition. While not positing Toynbee-type sweeping laws, Kennedy's account – again, targeting a particular kind of society and not societies in general, uses examples not only from Rome but also the British Empire, the Soviet Empire and potentially the contemporary United States, offers an intriguing typology that represents historical analysis applied on a global scale.

In later chapters we will invoke other works that, while again not really specifying unalterable laws of history, offer sweeping generalizations that world historians have assessed or that can be assessed as part of the analytical capacities world history programs can develop. Figuring out how to select and apply appropriate examples from the world history arsenal to test big generalizations, in sum, prompt students to use and build historical thinking skills.

A second angle – different from grand theories or historical laws, but also involving a testing process and the application of informed critical thinking – relates to analogies from one historical period to the next or from past to present. History can be seen as a vast laboratory of examples of human behavior, and it's possible that occasionally, perhaps often, situations occur today that closely resemble situations in the past, so that studying the earlier case might give us clues as to what's going on now, and as to how we should react. A recent example makes the point clearly. After the 9/11 terrorist attacks, the Bush administration moved quickly to make sure that Muslim Americans did not get targeted for reprisal. The administration clearly had in mind the World War II example in which Japanese Americans were rounded up and detained – a fear reaction that virtually everybody now agrees was profoundly unjust and unnecessary. The analogy: we know what not to do, because of the past, so let's be sure to be different.

The classic use of analogy in recent policy yields more complex results, however. In Munich in 1938, the leaders of Britain and France met with Hitler, who had just invaded parts of Czechoslovakia. Rather than threatening force against this aggression, they hoped that conciliation would work, and easily believed the Nazi leader's assurances that his appetites were satisfied. The British leader came back from Munich claiming he had achieved "peace in our time."

In fact, Hitler used the pause to ready a full takeover of Czechoslovakia, convinced that the Western allies would do nothing (and indeed it would take yet a third crisis, the invasion of Poland, to push them into action). Munich failed, and probably was the wrong strategy at the time; and all this was taken as a clear historical example – a clear analogical lesson – that appeasing aggressive dictators never works. In turn, this motivated American policies later on, in Korea, in Vietnam and even in dealing with Iraq's Saddam Hussein in the 1990s. Yet many historians would argue that this whole use of the Munich analogy, though understandable, was over-simple in terms of historical analysis, and profoundly misleading as a policy guide. Not all dictators are alike, not all harbor Hitler's unbounded territorial ambition; some might be open to constructive compromise. The policy aspects can be debated, but the history lesson should be clear: the attempt to use one past example as a guide to something later is fraught with difficulty, because it may assume more similarity between two different historical episodes than in fact exists. Testing analogies is intriguing, and it can be serious business.

World history students can explore how analogies have been used and they can learn to identify and test them in public discourse. In 2010, amid fears about the United States economy and a divisive and ineffective political process, several scholars and journalists returned to the analogy theme. One prominent article noted that the fall of Rome took shape in just a generation (this is highly debatable, however), and that the Ming dynasty and Soviet Russia under Gorbachev collapsed equally quickly (again, debatable). The conclusion? The United States might self-destruct before we have much time to do anything about it. Pure analogy: is it correct? Is it helpful?

THE HISTORICAL CORE: CHANGE OVER TIME

The central contribution of history as a discipline involves the understanding of processes of change, or at least the best possible approaches to an understanding of change. No other social science focuses on this phenomenon so explicitly, though many can contribute to relevant analysis. In turn, the most important habit of mind for students to advance in history programs – even more important than the assessment of evidence, though ideally both agendas can be embraced – involves grasping what the evaluation of change entails. The more experience students get in dealing with different kinds of change, with some guidance in applying the experience to the ongoing phenomenon of change, the better. For modern people are confronted with significant change around them, and with even more strident claims that change is occurring, whether the tag line is "things will never be the same" (i.e. I want you to believe that fundamental change is sweeping us off our feet) or "revolutionary new developments" (i.e. I want you to believe that things are getting better than ever). The capacity to deal with both the real issues of change and with the often inflated claims should be a fundamental goal of education, and this moves history to the front of the line.

Encounters with change in history can come up in several different ways. The most obvious is when a historian or some other observer specifically says: this or that behavior or institution changed greatly from this point onward. The claim invites assessment. More commonly, a historical account deals with a past leader or a major war or battle or a contested election and strongly implies that the result was a significant change. The claim here may be less explicit, but it too requires assessment. Or someone may simply wonder about an aspect of the present that seems to differ from the past, and ask the further question of when the key change set in: when did China become the kind of center for global manufacturing that it clearly is today, and what was involved in this process of change? Or, when and how did English begin to become something of a global language in various fields of endeavor? Questions about change in other words, may come up quite directly or they may be teased out of accounts of historical events or even biographies.

Analyzing change, in turn, has several components, and working on these components explicitly can accelerate the process of gaining competence in this crucial habit of mind:

If a change situation is presented, the first question is: change from what? *Establishing a baseline* is a vital element in dealing with change, because otherwise claims of change might turn out to be hollow assertions. Take an easy but illustrative case: in Western societies between 1880–1920, infant mortality rates began dropping well below traditional levels, creating a novel demographic regime and truly novel ingredients in the experience of families. In 1880, at least 20% of all children born would die before reaching age 2; in 1920 that figure (varying a bit by country among Western societies) was down to 5%. Putting the same point qualitatively: in 1880, most families could expect to experience at least one infant death, but in 1920 most families would be exempt. The baseline is clear, at 20%. Establishing baselines for less quantitatively-measurable changes is admittedly more difficult – but the approach at least can be defined. Thus a qualitative claim that, for example, the nature of war has fundamentally changed in the twentieth century should immediately invoke the response: *change from what? What are the key features that defined the nature of war previously?* And the same should apply to any change claim, whether it goes back in time – like the idea that the Renaissance dramatically changed European culture – or was just noticed yesterday.

A subset of the baseline question obviously calls for determination of the approximate date at which a change began to take hold. Historians can be annoyingly fussy about dates, and sometimes absolute precision is not as important as they like to think, but establishing key timeframes is essential to determine what change is all about.

These first analytical-empirical steps then call for three others:

(i)   First: was the change significant or trivial? (This involves once again an assessment of the baseline.) Pretty clearly, moving from common to uncommon, in infant mortality, is a significant change in human experience. But some other changes, though definable, don't pass a significance test. Take for example a French case, the Revolution of 1830, which despite the name was scarcely a revolution at all. The new regime moved from a pre-1830 elite with voting rights (100,000 eligible voters before the Revolution) to a larger elite (250,000 eligible voters), but this was simply not a very big deal. The wealthy still ruled France. The change is worth assessing, to be sure, but does not pass a crucial significance test. There is no magic definition of significance, and opinions should and will differ, but some notion of a test is vital, lest we drift into a chaos in which every small tweak in behavior is rated alongside fundamental shifts. Noisy events sometimes create great splash at the time, but turn out not to affect basic historical patterns in any dramatic way. Connecting historical specifics to the larger analysis of change and significance can be a challenging task, but it is an essential exercise in making history more than a set of rich stories.

(ii)   Second, once change is identified and its significance assessed: did the change continue in directions initially established, or was the trend, though still recognizable, adjusted as other factors entered the process? Japan enacted an important Education Act in 1872, and the resulting development of mass education was a vital and substantial change; but the way the change was first implemented, with guidance from lots of Western enthusiasts and advisers, and the way it was redirected in the 1880s toward a more nationalist and less individualist approach, was an important modification of trend. The operative word here is *process*: assessing change must involve more than comparing an end result to the initial baseline, because there are usually a number of permutations in between. It is really a question of seeing how, once a big change is launched, some smaller changes add relevant modifications.

(iii)   Finally, in dealing with all but quite recent history, it's important to ask if and when a particular change process draws to a close, presumably to be replaced either by another pattern of change or by essential stability. The advent of Islam, for example, was a huge change in world history, and for several centuries Islam spread to a variety of regions from its initial base in the Middle East. By 1500 however, though some further dissemination occurred, the process of diffusion slowed, and conversions to Islam as a force of change at a global level really trailed off at least until the nineteenth century (when new conversions began to occur in Africa). Islam remained a vital religious force, it still enters into discussions of world history after 1500, but the big change period was over in terms of Islamic impact on transforming wider world patterns. Attention after 1500 legitimately shifts to other major factors.

Exploring change has two other primary, standard components:

(1)   Any analysis of significant historical change almost inevitably deals with the causes involved. What factors generated the reduction in infant mortality rates? (It was not, surprisingly, primarily better medical care – the rise of pediatrics came later; but rather developments in public health, basic living standards, and probably also some shifts in parental attitudes, though harder to pin down, seem to have been largely responsible.) Figuring out causation puts change in larger historical context. It also gives greater meaning to change itself – if one knows *why* "something" is happening, one knows the something better as well. In the case of recent changes, where it might be desirable to consider improving on current outcomes, it's possible to moderate or redirect trends better when one knows what caused them in the first place.

Dealing with causes in history is a tricky subject, however. In contrast to laboratory science, historians cannot repeat experiments in order to say for sure that a given set of factors will inevitably generate standard results. Historical causes require debate, and they can relatively rarely be pinned down definitively. Uncertainty is not endless; certain factors may be proposed to explain change – like improvements in medical treatments, for the infant death rate issue – that can actually be proved not to apply. Timing is crucial: one of the reasons it's important to know pretty clearly *when* a change began is to help identify potentially relevant factors; features that occurred only after the change began obviously did not cause it, though they might further influence the trend pattern. It is often helpful to separate preconditions from active causes: Great Britain for example was able to generate the world's first industrial revolution in part because it had active holdings of iron and coal; but these resources clearly did not cause industrialization, because they'd been in the ground a long time; more active, time-specific causes must be sought. Comparison may help: if one society changes and another society, at least seemingly similarly situated, did not, then identifying the factors present in case one and absent in the other will help a lot. All of this is, however, demanding and challenging – ultimately, the hardest aspect of change for students to master. The issue must however be introduced, so that students learn how to approach the problem and learn to distinguish better from worse causation analysis (sometimes, as part of dealing with key historical controversies).

(2)   The final issue in dealing with change involves continuity. Rarely if ever – despite popular claims that something "changes everything" – does change obliterate previous patterns. Many individuals and societies demonstrate remarkable capacity to maintain prior patterns even amid change, or to combine them with change. Comparatively, some societies are more fiercely attached to preserving continuities than others, a key factor in world history at many points. Sometimes, in fact, continuity predominates over change, even for long stretches of time. Dealing with continuity, seeing how it combines with change, figuring out what causes promote continuity, even when some shifts are occurring – all this forms a vital target for historical analysis as part of the larger commitment to exploring change.

Classic invitations for tests for continuity involve major revolutions. The Russian Revolution of 1917, for example, unquestionably brought huge changes to Russian politics, society and culture, and some revolutionaries believed that ultimately everything would be transformed. But the conscientious historian notes that along with change, the new Russian government quickly established a secret police apparatus which, though renamed, showed strong similarities to its tsarist counterpart. Continuity even more obviously accompanied the American Revolution of the eighteenth century, including the maintenance of slavery in the South. Even the most systematic efforts to redefine human life can and should be evaluated in terms of vital remnants of prior patterns.

HEADLINERS FOR HABITS OF MIND

Interpreting documents:

- What questions can they be used to answer?
- Are they shaped by particular points of view?
- How can they be used to build arguments?
- How would additional evidence help?

Confronting differing interpretations:

- How do they use evidence?
- Do they display particular bias?
- How logical are the arguments?

Change over time:

- Baseline: what were the patterns prior to change?
- Level of significance
- Timing: start and stop of the change process
- Process: additional modifications, wider consequences
- Causation
- Continuities

Comparison:

- Establishing the comparative problem
- Comparing subtopics
- Causes of similarities and differences
- Conclusion: main similarities and differences

Local/Global:

- How do local and global factors serve as causes of an event or process?
- Comparing local factors in two cases to explore different combinations with a global factor

The checklist for dealing with change – for forming the appropriate habits of mind—thus involves a manageable sequence. Once the change theme emerges, either through direct claims or a desire to assess the results of a major historical event, the first step is to determine *timing* and *baseline*. This then moves into discussion of *significance*, into an understanding of change as an accumulating *process* that may pick up additional ingredients, and into some determination of when the active change period ends. Dealing with *causation* is often directly invited, and any full evaluation of change and process must pick up on the causes involved. Finally, the *change–continuity* balance requires explicit attention.

Students in world history courses can expect to deal with various types of change and should practice using a checklist for items like baseline or ongoing continuity. It is also helpful to recognize the types of change that particularly preoccupy world historians – that connect their subject area to the larger agenda of learning how better to assess change and to develop habits of mind that can be utilized outside and inside the classroom. World historians are deeply interested in changes in *systems of interconnections* – trade patterns, migration, missionary travel, disease transmission – plus additions or subtractions of societies involved in these systems. *Shifts in power balances* within the contact systems are also relevant – the rise of the Arabs, for example, by the seventh century, or the later surge of the Chinese in the early fifteenth century. *Alterations in basic economic and technology systems*, and their ramifications, are a key focus in defining big-picture changes in the human experience. Redefinitions of basic aspects of social activity, such as warfare, on a global or at least multiregional level, sometimes relate to the transformations of larger systems – e.g. the impacts of industrialization on war – but may sometimes have independent characteristics. Big shifts in *population structures*, with attendant results like new migration patterns, are clearly on the list. Finally, *patterns of change and continuity within major societies*, once an initial cultural and institutional base is set, command wide attention.

WORLD HISTORY HABITS OF MIND

There are at least two types of habits of mind that are particularly attached to world history, and not history in general. They are not necessarily more important than the other categories – indeed, exploring change through world history may have a commanding position – but they certainly require explicit attention. Comparison is one facet; relating global to local factors is the other.

DEVELOPING COMPARISON

Comparing two or more societies is one of the connective tissues of world history. Almost any injunction toward global education urges students to gain some sense of how different cultures operate, and while this can degenerate into a long list of separate descriptions, it gains logic when it is implemented through comparative analysis. And this analysis, in turn, seeks to explore what's different about key societies, at particular points in time and in reaction to roughly common stimuli, and what's basically similar.

Not all comparisons are relevant to world history. To be applicable, the comparison must focus on a significant aspect of at least two societies, often over a considerable time span. An ideal candidate would be two societies' reactions to the same factor: how did early modern China and early modern India compare in their policies toward trade with Western merchants?

People compare all the time, obviously. We compare teachers, or professional athletes, or acquaintances. But comparison in a world history setting goes beyond the normal experience, and needs clear highlighting. It requires not only some knowledge about each of the two (or more) cases but enough assimilation of that knowledge that the cases can be actively brought together, and not simply treated sequentially. Students often misstep in their comparative work by discussing one society, then another with at most a tiny comparative reference at the end – leaving the active task of comparison in fact to the faculty reader. This is juxtaposition, and not analysis. Comparative analysis needs to be set up explicitly, stating or restating the problem so that both cases (and all cases, if there are more than two) are embraced at the outset. Illustrative material needs to be subdivided so that the societies are compared on each major sub-point. Students who mention themes for one case without establishing how they operate (or don't exist) in the other case are not following real comparative guidelines.

The checklist for comparative thinking is not as elaborate as the sequence for dealing with change over time, but it does offer criteria. The initial introduction of the comparison should itself be comparative, often forecasting whether differentiation or similarity will provide the more important organizing principle. The topic should then be broken down into component parts, each of them permitting a comparison. Sometimes (as with change over time) attention to the *causes* of similarity or difference will actively aid the analysis. Finally, a conclusion should directly re-confront the basic comparative issues, tallying the balance between similarity and difference.

Example: compare Confucian and Islamic approaches to women during the postclassical period. Wrong: offer a solid treatment of the major relevant features of the *Quran*, and then turn to Chinese materials. Wrong: discuss property rights for women in Islam but ignore the same topic for Confucianism. Right: establish an overall comparative framework at the outset, then deal with spiritual position (both cases), marriage and divorce patterns (both cases), property (both cases), cultural status and education (both cases), and so on, capped by a firmly comparative overall conclusion.

While a single formula would be misleading, there are some standard features to a presentation. A comparison begins with a statement of the topic, dealing with all the societies involved and never starting out with a single case alone. While students may need to provide some separate context for each case subsequently, most of the ensuing presentation should be comparative, breaking into subtopics. Again, some attention to causation of similarities and differences might often be involved. And a final comparative conclusion would conclude the effort.

Comparison, in other words, requires active thought and some standard organizational techniques, and these can be accelerated, made more routine, not only with repeated experience in classroom discussion or exercises, but also with explicit awareness of the main structural requirements.

Comparison in world history offers a few other hazards, though all of them can be overcome. If one's own society is part of the comparison, or even if one of the societies involved seems more like one's own than the other, some suspension of attachment is required, and it's not always easy. By the standards of the contemporary West there's a temptation to an almost visceral reaction to practices in other societies like (until fairly recently) foot binding for many women in China, or veiling in the Middle East. If comparison involves these practices, starting out with a simple condemnation is not likely to be very helpful. The challenge of maintaining one's principles but not tripping over them in cross-cultural comparison is quite real, and it's arguably a useful byproduct of the larger comparative endeavor.

Ideally, indeed, some experience in comparison should also allow one to understand why practices in one's own society might be viewed askance by other cultures. Asking, for example, what features of the

West a nineteenth-century Russian or Japanese observer might have found particularly misguided is a legitimate comparative question, but it takes knowledge, a certain amount of confidence, and real comparative experience to address (unless, of course, one comes from a culture outside the West). Many prescriptions for global competence include a category on understanding how other societies might view one's own, which is easier said than done: but comparative experience at least makes the task imaginable.

World history comparisons require equal openness to similarity and to difference. In practice, because so many textbook materials emphasize the separate experience and distinctive cultural attributes of key societies, students are often tempted to identify differences most readily. Similarities often involve probing a bit beneath the surface. In the classical period, for example, Hinduism and Confucianism seem very different, and they certainly were in many respects. Hinduism supported a caste system, which Confucianism did not; Hinduism was a religion with a deeply spiritual component, and Confucianism differed here as well. Both belief systems, however, supported social inequality (even if in different specific forms) and had at least an implicit purpose the maintenance of good order despite significant gaps among social levels. Similarities result not simply from the important fact that humans are humans and develop some common responses, but also from the fact that, in key periods, different societies grapple with common problems – such as the challenge, in the classical period, of establishing cultures that would help draw together large geographical territories. There's no automatic balance between similarity and difference; the point, in comparison, is to test both aspects.

Comparison, finally, must not be static. Societies may be more similar at some points, more dissimilar at others as they respond to different factors or differentially to the same factor. Common global processes – for example the new interregional trade levels in the early modern period – generate different reactions from different participants, and these differences can engender other comparative complexities over time. A comparative formulation for India and China in one period does not necessarily apply to another. Change (and continuity) must be combined with the comparative effort over time. This requires still more knowledge and analysis than static comparisons involve, and if requested prematurely can be overwhelming. But the capacity to aim for is clear nevertheless.

The goal of experience in comparison, as in handling sources or dealing with change over time, is to develop a capacity and recognition that ultimately transcend the classroom. Global news stories are replete with implicit invitations to comparison and even more statements about national superiority or distinctiveness that in fact can only be substantiated through comparison. Recognition that comparison is required, even to make full sense of any single society, is the first step, and world history programs provide that and more.

THE LOCAL AND THE GLOBAL

This is the final analytical category that springs directly from the world history agenda. As scholars contemplate globalization today, they argue that human lives are increasingly determined by interactions between global and local or regional factors. American consumer patterns, around behaviors that have evolved nationally like Christmas buying frenzies, strongly shape production decisions in China, and vice versa, to take an easy example. World historians urge that these kinds of interactions, though arguably more intense today, are not new, but can be traced at various points in world history. That tracing, in turn, provides both data and experience to handle the wider-reaching global-local combinations that operate at present.

Too often, world history statements stipulate the local-global combination as part of the habits of mind agenda, but then fail to follow up. It's not an easy analytical category to break down, at least on first glance. In fact, however, it really focuses several habits of mind elements that have already been covered. It's mainly the label that is new.

First, the local and global mixture invites attention to the complex causation of change. The basic argument is that new combinations of local and global inputs will prompt observable shifts in patterns of behavior. Some components of the combination may involve continuity: in the example above, American Christmas habits began to emerge in the nineteenth century and basically persist today though more opulently; the new element is the global production angle. Local-global analysis is simply a special case of causation analysis.

It may also, however, involve some comparison. Global influences – emanating, say, from another culture – can be compared with prior local habits to help determine how great a jolt a new juncture will be, and what reactions might ensue. In the late nineteenth century, for example, new Western pressures on East Asia, primarily to insist on greater access to markets, drew measurably different responses from Japan than from China. Japanese leaders could remember earlier successful imitations, and Chinese leaders could not. Comparing local factors – including in this case the different kinds of historical experience with interacting with foreign influences but also some differences in prior understandings of what the West was all about – helps explain the contrasts in local–global equations. Causation analysis, supplemented by a relevant comparative sense, should do the trick. The target is both a better grasp of global factors as they actually operate, and not simply in the abstract, but an understanding of local developments, and local variety, as well.

The local–global approach can encompass some major historical developments, and not just recent ones. The new patterns of the Atlantic slave trade beginning in the sixteenth century, from West Africa to the Americas, depended on prior local traditions of slave-holding and newer local motivations of African merchants and rulers eager to earn money and acquire new goods such as guns. But the patterns depended also on the dramatic population declines in the Americas and the resultant need for new cheap labor (another regional development), on the capacities of European shipping, and on European eagerness for new profits that clearly overrode any cultural hesitations about seizing distant people as slaves. Here were local–global interactions with huge consequences for three major regions – Africa, the Americas and Europe – and for millions of individual lives.

The local–global combination, finally, itself needs to be seen as part of world-historical change. Clearly, the global part of the combination has tended to become more important in each suc-ceeding historical period, though local–global combinations of some sorts are not purely modern phenomena. Looking at how global factors expand their reach, thanks to new technologies and new outreach policies, is a fundamental part of the larger explora-tion of change and continuity – but without ever forgetting that, even in the globalized world of the early twenty-first century, the local still leaves a strong mark.

CONCLUSION

Many students come into a world history program with relatively little analytical experience, either in historical thinking generally or in the special context provided by world history. They don't, for example, spontaneously seize on comparison, tending to prefer – not only because it seems easier, but because it corresponds to their prior experience in looking at societies individually – to take things one by one.

For their part, some world history instructors don't manage to articulate their analytical goals for a course as explicitly as might be desired. They want students to learn to compare, or to deal with change over time in global context, but they don't directly say so and they don't talk in any detail about the approaches that work best. It's one thing to assign a comparative essay on a good topic. It's another to discuss the key stages of comparative analysis and the differences between active comparison and mere juxtaposition or sequence. The same applies to change over time, with opportunities to explore directly what it means to establish a baseline or how to weigh significance. There's no simple set of formulas for the habits of mind world history involves, and there's every reason to encourage actual experience, in class discussions and various types of assignments. But there are ways to accelerate the identification and acquisition of key habits of mind.

And this is why, going into a world history course, awareness of what kinds of analytical capacities underlie the learning experience in world history is unusually desirable. Key assignments will expose students to relevant types of source assessment or the interaction between local and global causation. For students, knowing what to look for, how the habits of mind are defined and how they can be broken down into stages or steps, is a key element in stepping up to the challenge.

Balance is an important aspect of the habits of mind approach. A world history project that worked only on documents assessment, or only on comparison, would be falling short. Not every item of the list requires attention, but there should be a mix, and explicit encounters with analysis of change, comparison, and the local–global are standard components of any good program.

Always, again, the hope is that students will emerge from a world history course with some analytical impulses they didn't have before, or didn't have as fully developed – impulses that will continue to serve in life after class in dealing with and making sense of ongoing global developments. Recognizing when a newscaster is claiming a major change (whether the term is used or not) or when a blog can be evaluated only through comparison, and knowing what to do next to gain greater understanding and perspective, is a real boon, in work and informed citizenship alike. Regrettably, some world history facts may fade from memory – though hopefully not all of them. Core habits of mind can be regularly exercised and can actively persist.

FURTHER READING

Several useful general works on historical habits of mind include: Sam Wineburg's *Historical Thinking and Other Unnatural Acts: Charting the Future of Teaching the Past* (Philadelphia: Temple University Press, 2001); and *Knowing, Teaching, and Learning History: National and International Perspectives* by Peter N. Stearns, Peter Seixas, and Sam Wineburg (New York: NYU Press, 2001). The National Center for History in the Schools (http://nchs. ucla.edu/) and the National Standards for World History (http://www. sscnet.ucla.edu/nchs/wrldtoc.html) also provide good overviews. Diverse interpretation is covered well by Robert B. Bain in several articles, including "AP World History Habits of Mind: Reflecting on World History's Unique Challenge to Students' Thinking," In *Teacher's Guide: AP World History* (Princeton, NJ: College Entrance Examination Board, 2000).

MANAGING TIME
CHOOSING AND EVALUATING WORLD HISTORY PERIODS

In Chapter 2, basic features of the main world history periods were laid out. But the thinking behind selection of periods was not explicitly discussed. Understanding this thinking is crucial to dealing actively with world history materials. Selection of periods, and assessing this selection, constitute vital elements of the kinds of habits of mind world history promotes – particularly in the category of change over time.

To a student encountering them for the first time, world history periods can seem both abstract and arbitrary. The purpose of this chapter is to go over the criteria used in choosing the periods and to reemphasize how the periods, or rather their definitions, can be applied to organizing and in many ways simplifying world history data. Debate is part of this process as well. Almost all the periods have important flaws and messiness: they were not decreed by some divine hand, but rather devised by historians and open to discussion or revision. Here too is a component of developing appropriate habits of mind – including willingness to deal with controversy – and directing them to one of the essential building blocks of historical scholarship.

WHAT PERIODIZATION IS ALL ABOUT

For periodization is the way historians try to capture the process of change and make it intelligible to themselves and others, unless they are simply content to tell stories about past battles or elections or show trials. Periodization assumes – and this assumption itself deserves some discussion – that change is neither random nor constant, but that, at certain points in time, factors converge to change the basic context for the ways societies operate. This process creates a new or substantially new framework that marks the beginning of a definable novel chunk of time – a new period, in short.

Historians who believe in deeper and more definable patterns of change – and most world historians fall into this category – look for at least two, and often three, types of measurements that allow periods to be defined.

Assumption #1 in a periodization scheme: themes that had prevailed before the new period begins recede in importance or may even be reversed. A new period does not avoid some continuity from the past, so it is misleading to expect every feature to change, but it does require that the previous framework loses its dominance – otherwise, it must be assumed that the previous period continues to operate. In terms of thinking about change, this first assumption establishes a baseline.

Assumption #2 in a periodization scheme then follows by necessity: if the previous organizing principles fade in importance, or are even replaced, then it becomes essential to define what the new themes are, and how they begin to organize key facets of the human experience. At some point, even the new themes will begin to lose force, yielding yet another period and requiring the same kind of analysis inherent in assumption #1.

Defining and assessing periods, then, involves identifying basic themes in whatever historical subject area is being evaluated, and determining how one set of themes at some point yields to another. Testing any historian's periodization focuses primarily on the adequacy of this determination, deciding whether a good case is made that one framework gives way to another.

Many world history periods offer a third kind of identification, when the end of one period and the launch of another is triggered or at least heralded by some dramatic event or process. World War I – unquestionably a huge event – is thus seen as a turning point in a whole variety of historical exercises, including most world history formulations. A big event is not an absolutely essential feature of a successful periodization scheme (sometimes basic changes sneak up more quietly), and not all big events actually yield fundamental, durable changes. Too much emphasis on convenient markers can be misleading. But when a major event or collection of events summarizes or causes basic change, it certainly makes periodization analysis clearer.

Sometimes, choosing or evaluating a period may not require a lot of thought. Any history of modern Japan, for example, will almost certainly identify a period running from the mid-1920s until 1945 in which military authorities dominated the political and diplomatic scene. Pre-1920s features of Japanese history, some of them running well back in time to the culture of the post-classical samurai, helped prepare the new period – but the level of military control was measurably different from the framework of the previous Meiji era, in part because of developments and frustrations during World War I. And without question Japan's loss of World War II, and the subsequent occupation period, yielded a much different assessment of military motives and structures that continues to define aspects of the Japanese experience even today. Even this fairly tidy framework for determining a distinctive period in Japanese militarism should not be accepted without some testing, particularly on the early end of the process, but it emerges pretty clearly in most formulations.

Three common complexities must be noted in periodization schemes, even in relatively easy cases. First – and this follows directly from the previous chapter's discussion of change and continuity – a new framework in place does not mean that there is no relevant subsequent change, prior to a period's ending outright. Change as a process continues, even with the new framework installed. Japanese militarism was not a constant from the 1920s until 1945. The notion of a basic period of authoritarian military control makes sense, but the early stages differed from the intensifications of the later 1930s. Periods, in other words, embrace internal changes, but so long as these don't overturn the framework – and this is often a judgment call, which can and should be debated – the periodization schema survives.

Second, a period in one subject area does not assure a definable new pattern in other areas. History is not so tidy. Identifying a new political framework does not necessarily have much applicability to changes in gender relations or manufacturing – it may, but the connection must be verified and not merely asserted. Even big-ticket markers, like World War I, do not extend to all crucial areas, though historians, to save trouble, sometimes use conventional dates of this sort to suggest change across the board. The events between 1914–18, and the factors that led up to them, legitimately designate change in the nature of warfare, in Europe's position in the world, in Middle Eastern politics, in nationalism and imperialism, even in domestic political structures and movements. But they're not particularly decisive dates for the history of women. To be sure, World War I prompted some new use of women in factories, but this proved temporary; it helped to move women's voting rights forward in a few countries (the United States, Britain, Turkey, Germany and the Soviet Union) but not in any sense uniformly even within Europe. Feminism overall did not advance, and in some ways retreated a bit. The war should be considered in women's history, but it did not shape fundamental or sweeping change save in the few countries literally swept up in a revolutionary process as a corollary of the conflict itself. Women's history has a periodization too – just a somewhat different one from that applicable to global military and political life.

A final complexity – at least in many crucial instances – involves the messiness inherent in determining precise beginning and ending points of key periods, the need to deal with fuzziness in transitions even when a new period can ultimately be defined fairly clearly. Often, for example, a new set of ideas will pop up, suggesting the beginning of some novel developments; but it will take some time for them to gain any sort of wide acceptance and begin to influence behaviors. It was late in the seventeenth century, for example, in the Western world, that thinkers like John Locke began to argue the novel proposition that children did not have built-in characteristics, but rather were "blank slates" whose mental apparatus would largely be developed or distorted by learning. Here, as a seed, was the inception point of new commitments to education, an attack on older Christian ideas about children shaped by original sin, a potentially distinctive take on childhood in general. But it would take well over a century for these ideas to gain much influence on actual practices concerning children, by parents or educational authorities or political reformers. So when does a new period in the history of childhood begin: with the core new ideas or with more extensive implementations? Clearly, a bit of both, and the existence of a century or more of complicated transition simply has to be built into the periodization scheme. Similar fuzziness can be attached to big-ticket periodizations such as the industrial revolution. It's quite easy to determine the dates of major new technologies, like the steam engine or key innovations in textile manufacturing equipment. But it took a long time for the inventions to translate into measurable changes in national economies, even in pioneering industrializers like Great Britain or Belgium, and longer still for wider social implications to become clear. So when does the industrial period of history begin? It could be the mid-eighteenth century, to capture the first new inventions, or a full century later, to capture the measurable advent of industrial societies (it was in 1850 that the British population became half-urban for example, the first such development in world history), or even a bit later still if the world outside the West is to be considered.

To sum up: periodization assumes that at certain crucial points, patterns once dominant yield to different patterns. The crucial task of introducing periodization correspondingly focuses on identifying what the prior patterns were and when and how they began to change, and then identifying the new themes that replace them. Sometimes this task is further clarified by the existence of major events or landmarks that either cause the replacement of one framework by another, or offer symbolic evidence that a shift is underway. Even in the clearest cases, periodization must be complicated by an understanding that further changes will occur, as trends take hold and react to other forces, and by a realization that not all human behaviors respond to the same factors, so that periods must vary depending on subject matter. Often, finally, complexity is deepened by the fact that important periods rarely spring full-grown at a single date, so that transitions leading into a period and then, later, leading away toward a new set of developments have to be built into the analysis.

Periodization, clearly, requires thought, and even when a student of history is evaluating someone else's periodization, rather than generating a schema in the first place, thoughtfulness remains essential. Periodization invites careful identification of the assumptions involved, from the transition from one set of patterns to another to the issue of figuring out how many facets of history can be embraced by any one periodization model. The result is a more intelligent and active appreciation of how change occurs. The result also, however, is an understanding that periodization efforts are constructed by scholars and students of history, not magically determined by some divine hand, and can always be contested and debated.

MOVING PERIODIZATION INTO WORLD HISTORY

The discussion in Chapter 2, in presenting key features of the periodization schemes used in world history, made it clear that periodization is one of the fundamental ways historians make the vast domain of world history coherent and manageable. With periodization it is not necessary to move century by century, but to see larger frameworks, some of which last for a considerable duration. With periodization, it is possible to identify some key points at which frameworks change, and to discuss the factors and complexities involved in these transitions.

Because world history periodization is of necessity broad, involving big sweeps of time, it inevitably reproduces the various kinds of complexities noted above. Messy inceptions and terminations are inescapable. Rarely does a period emerge suddenly or in clear cut fashion, which means transitions both in beginnings and endings are almost always part of the equation – along with debates over what specific dates are best. Some periods, to be sure, are tidier than others; it will be tempting to see modern units as more quickly defined than earlier cases, though this may be misleading. Never, however, does a single focal event set a periodization process in motion at the world history level. Even World War I is just part of a larger accumulation of factors.

World history periods are also thematically varied. Never does a period embrace all aspects of the human experience equally well – some periods are defined particularly by developments in trade and cultural life, with less precise political shape, while in others cultural definitions are hard to come by. Thus trans-regional political patterns are hard to discern for the postclassical period – which does not mean there were no political developments – just that they have to be traced primarily within specific regions. In contrast shared cultural trends were largely lacking from the early modern centuries, despite crucial innovations in several specific regions.

World history periodization, in other words, puts the thematic diversity of the whole periodization enterprise into vivid relief. Very few themes constantly crop up; even basic technological innovations do not always enter into core definitions.

In addition, a grasp of basic periods must be supplemented by understanding the various trends and enhancements that occur within the period itself; world history periods are never static. Here, to be sure, presentations will vary depending on the amount of time available for detail. Ultimately, for example, the formation of major empires was one of the key emblems of the classical period. But not only did the specific nature of empires vary, depending on region, chronology varied as well. The imperial form emerged quickly in Persia; but in China, India and the Mediterranean, empires developed only after long exposure to more localized political units. If time permits, tracing how this happened is a significant part of the classical story, without contradicting the ultimate insistence that political integration through empire became a defining feature of the classical period as a whole.

And world history periods involve another variable, that more precise, single-region periodization schemes may largely avoid: the variable of geography. There are both positive and negative aspects here. The negative: few if any world history periodization schemes work equally well for all parts of the world. This is inescapably true until recent times, but the problem persists even today. Noting geographic exceptions, regions that have to be taken up on a more case by case basis, simply have to complicate the basic periodization schemes. But world history periodization – and this is the positive aspect – must pass a geography test. The basic themes of any world history period must apply (though quite possibly in regionally distinctive ways) to a number of different areas and societies, and not just to one or two. (An interesting challenge for world history students when they get to the contemporary period is to make sure they don't over-rely on trends they're aware of in their own country, assuming somehow that since the trends are important to them, they must be global; the multi-regional test cannot be based on parochial assumptions.) The frameworks of world history periodization are useful precisely because they designate themes to which many societies had to respond. The result is a combination of shared patterns and of opportunities for comparison that decisively prevent world history from becoming simply a catalogue of one uncon- nected regional history after another.

Despite all the complexities, two other vital features stand out in dissecting world history periodization. First, the points of funda- mental change are not numerous. The agricultural and industrial revolutions, the impact of iron, the acceleration of interregional contacts around 1000 CE and again around 1500 — this is a man- ageable list. A slightly more detailed periodization scheme can be built around it, as we saw in Chapter 2.

The second guideline for world history periodization highlights the presence of two factors in virtually every schema, at least from 1000 BCE onward. Each world history period involves measurable changes in the *nature and range of trading interactions* (often with relevant technology changes attached), and each period involves measurable changes in the *roster and balance among major societies or civilizations.*

Shifts in contact patterns are fundamental. The classical period, ultimately involving new levels of interregional trade along Silks Roads and through the Indian Ocean, obviously contrasts with the more diffuse and irregular interactions of the river valley civilizations and other societies; the post-classical redefined levels, routes and technologies of trade, and these were defined yet again by the global patterns emerging after 1500. Industrial production levels and technologies generated yet another level by the long nineteenth century, and so on. Note: the emphasis on the changes in contact patterns as a fundamental criterion for world history periodization also means that in each new period the balance between the local and the global shifts somewhat, in favor of the latter — though some transitions, like the post-classical, are more important than others.

Power balances may sound crude, and some world historians, eager to give each region its due, may shy away from this criterion. But the rise of large states and culture zones in the classical period, considerably balanced, but with some special importance to the role of South Asia, contrasts obviously with the development of the Arab world and Islam as arguably the first "world-class" civilization in the postclassical centuries. This was then ultimately replaced by the rise of the West but amid considerable regional equilibrium in the early modern period followed by the brief decades of Western industrial control that help define the long nineteenth century. World War I and the twentieth century then launch a gradual and complex unseating of Western dominance, helping to shape the contemporary period in turn.

Trade and exchange patterns and power balances never work in isolation: depending on the period they may be supplemented by cultural factors (like the spread of world religions in the postclassical centuries) or social changes (the decline of slavery during the long nineteenth century, or shifts in population levels) or political alterations like the pervasiveness of empires during the early modern age. But it simplifies the quest for the motors of world history periodization to know that two criteria, over the past 3000 years, have always been involved. When a period is introduced, in other words, look for what changes occur in trade patterns and inter-societal balances, and then ask what other factors join with these two categories to give shape to the new period overall and to differentiate it from what went before. World history periodization is not made simple as a result, but it's not a brand new menu of social ingredients every time. And the most fundamental shifts: agriculture, iron, new levels of interaction, and industrialization contribute in turn, particularly to patterns of exchange. World history periodization, in other words, has an analytical structure that is hardly random and that is not impossibly detailed.

The extent of coherence in world history periodization imposes some caution. One world historian has emphasized how hard it is to pretend to integrate most key phenomena into one list of periods and why "a periodization that seems illuminating to one scholar is wrongheaded to another." Despite all this, there is in fact considerable agreement on the big markers, and involvement in world history does not require incessant dispute or massive uncertainty about the patterns of change or time. Each period should be hauled out for critical evaluation – this is really important – but there is no need to incorporate constant controversy.

CHECKLIST ON PERIODIZATION

(1) Have the themes of the prior period been noted, and a change in their nature or importance identified?

(2) (a) Have the themes of the new period been identified? Are there related shifts in technology and demography? (b) Are shifts in

power balances and contact patterns identified? What other new
themes must be added to these?

(3) Are there marker events or processes both at beginning and end
of the period, and if not are the signs of change adequate anyway?

(4) Is there clear evidence that the new periodization applies to a
number of societies and regions, not just one or two?

Secondary list:

(1) Are there important topics to which this particular periodization
does *not* apply?

(2) (a) Are there some regions or societies to which the periodization
does *not* apply? (b) What are the main comparative differences in
regional responses to the new comparative framework?

(3) Are there some transitional complexities at the beginning or end
of period, or both?

(4) Are there alternative options that might be advanced instead of
this periodization?

IMPLEMENTING WORLD HISTORY PERIODIZATION: THE EARLY PHASES

Periodization has a serious and constructive purpose, in helping to
focus on main themes of change in any historical subject area. It
calls on analytical capacities, to see how the themes impact various
activities or regions, and to sort through the inevitable complexities
of fuzzy transitions and change processes once a period's framework
is initially established. In world history, periodization helps highlight particularly important and sweeping points of change, and also
calls attention to recurrent redefinitions of trade and exchange systems
and power balances. Understanding what goes into periodization
decisions helps manage and sort historical data, providing extensive
though by definition not permanent coherences. Periodization also
sets up key comparative issues, in figuring out how different societies
responded to basic themes.

Actually translating periodization principles into world history
coverage both illustrates the general features of the technique and

provides some additional cautions and guidelines. Issues in the many thousands of years in the early human experience differ from those in the past three millennia.

Question one, which has gained vigorous new attention recently, is very simply: where to begin world history? In the old days, history survey inceptions usually emphasized the advent of writing, distinguishing between prehistory (a subject for archeology more than history in these formulations) and real history on the basis of written records. This distinction has largely dropped from view, and most world history programs begin now with some brief discussion of human origins and migrations, and the nature of the hunting and gathering economy, as a backdrop to the first systematic change in the human experience with the advent of agriculture.

Beginning tentatively in the 1980s, and emerging with greater gusto in the past decade, an alternative approach has emerged that adopts the deliberately grand label of "big history" and seeks to incorporate world history in a far larger chronological and topical vision. Big history advocates urge attention to the whole history of the universe, all 13-plus billion years of it. They start with the Big Bang, move to the creation of the first stars; the emergence of life becomes the fifth stage of an ultimately eight-part scenario, the advent of the human species the sixth, agriculture the seventh and the arrival of industrial modernity the final stage to date. The goal is to seek common themes and patterns without full distinction between the human experience and the earlier and ongoing evolution of larger physical and biological systems. The field embraces biology, climatology, archeology and obviously population and environmental studies. This interdisciplinarity is one of big history's selling points. A host of different time scales are involved, though a disproportionate amount of attention does go to the emergence and activities of humans. Big history scholars and teachers argue that understanding ourselves is possible only through exposure to the "largest story of all." Big history has eager advocates, but whether it will generate new standards for the early phases of most world history programs remains to be seen.

The challenge of big history aside, several other issues confront world history programs in dealing with the early phases of the human experience. Manageability is a consideration here; lack of systematic information inhibits a full deployment of the kind of periodization scheme feasible from the classical era onward; and the disjuncture of key developments in time and in geographical space produces constraints. Some key points, furthermore, are not yet entirely clear. We don't know, for example, exactly when the capacity for speech emerged, with estimates varying by as much as 50,000 years. Nor do we know the processes by which *Homo sapiens sapiens* emerged as sole human species, as against other advanced human types like the Neanderthal.

Evidence of patterns that help demarcate later historical periods is also frustratingly elusive. We know that hunting and gathering groups not only migrated but periodically interacted, setting up types of contact that might be compared with later, more systematic types of exchange. But it's often hard to get beyond the simple statement that contacts occasionally occurred. We know, for example, that sometime between 30,000 and 15,000 BCE, humans some place in Africa or Asia invented the bow and arrow, a considerable advance in hunting and military technology in allowing killing at a distance. We know that the technology spread, ultimately reaching virtually every part of Asia, Africa and Europe. At some point it also crossed to the Americas, where it began very gradually to move southward. By the time Columbus arrived in 1492 Native Americans throughout North America (including Aztecs in Central America) and in the northern parts of South America understood and used the bow and arrow – but Incas, a bit farther south in the Andes, had not yet acquired the weapons. (Australian natives were left out of this particular exchange process altogether.) How did transmissions of this sort occur, and why were they sometimes slow and limited? Similar questions arise about possible early trading activities. There is evidence that bananas – native to present-day Indonesia – had reached the island of Madagascar by 1000 BCE, but we don't know for sure if they had also penetrated Africa itself that early, and we don't know what kind of trade and travel brought them even part way across the Indian Ocean. We know, in sum, that exchanges occurred early on, an obvious sign the people understood their advantages at least occasionally, but we know far too little about them to offer a clear baseline for later types of interaction that were both more extensive and more abundantly documented.

AGRICULTURE AND CIVILIZATION

Opportunities for periodization obviously improve greatly with the great agricultural revolution. Settled communities began to leave larger amounts of material evidence for later analysis, including more varied works of art but also materials used in production and trade. The emergence of civilizations as forms of human organization amplified evidence even further, and the overall river valley civilization period, from 3500 to about 1200 or 1000 BCE, can be broken down into much more precise statements about changes and continuities in particular societies like Mesopotamia and Egypt, where periodization schemes are quite elaborate.

Constraints remain, however. Far more is known about the Middle East and North Africa than about Harappa or even early China, which hampers larger statements about world history developments in the early civilization period. Timing of major developments varied considerably still by region. While Shang dynasty China fits the river valley civilization model, it emerged quite a bit later than earlier exemplars farther west – just as dates of initial agriculture had varied greatly by region. Similarly, because of the pronounced separation of most regional developments, it's difficult to generalize much about the end of the river valley period. The collapse of Harappan society and then the influx and very gradual adaptation of Indo-Europeans hunter-gatherers contrasts with the smoother transition from river valley to early classical in China, which was different again from the gradual decline of the Egyptian kingdom. Using roughly 1000 BCE to mark the transition from river valley to classical is really just a date of convenience, not a solid periodization boundary that cuts across regional differences.

Finally, periodization discussions in the early period, after the advent of agriculture and even civilization, are always constrained by the need to keep in mind the continued viability and importance of alternative systems, and particularly the nomadic economies. Here, detailed periodization schemes don't work well at all, save when the migrations or invasions of a particular nomadic group, like the Indo-Europeans or the Huns, broke into the historical record of other societies. Yet key nomadic areas not only existed but could generate considerable historical impact. They constitute another sign of the human and regional variability that complicate any periodization statements into fairly recent times.

IMPLEMENTING WORLD HISTORY PERIODIZATION: THE LATER PHASES

Periodization difficulties hardly crumble away with the development of the great classical societies, but they begin to take on different contours. Evidence improves; regional variety, though still great, diminishes a bit particularly in key parts of Africa, Asia and Europe; patterns of exchange and balance among major societies begin to provide the markers that permit more coherent analysis.

CLASSICAL PERIOD

What was happening, at least by 500 BCE, was the development of some new parallelisms among major areas in Asia, southern Europe and North Africa, based on the use of iron tools and weapons and the related opportunities for expanded regional zones of operation. The emergence of more regular and identifiable interregional trading connections, among the same areas, allows much clearer analysis of this aspect of world history periodization. Even as major regions were defining very different sets of characteristics, world history patterns were becoming clearer, which in turn allows for meaningful and extensive use of periodization techniques.

The classical period echoes, to be sure, some of the earlier issues. The classical societies hardly embraced the whole world, which limits the coverage of classical periodization. Large stretches of northern Europe and much of sub-Saharan Africa moved according to different dynamics, where key themes involve the spread of agriculture or new movements of peoples, as in the great Bantu migrations or the arrival of Slavic peoples in new sections of east central Europe. The Americas, also, followed unconnected patterns (the Olmec period and then the early Mayans, in the case of Central America) that again are interesting and important but that do not fit a periodization scheme based on the patterns of the classical societies.

The fact that, even for the major societies, the classical period begins without major trans-regional events or signals (though the impact of the Indo-Europeans on India and also the Middle East and southern Europe counts for something), adds more than the usual transitional complexity to this aspect of analysis. The end of the period is more definable, with the common involvement with new challenges of invasion, societal decline, and disease – but, just to remind us all that world history is hardly conveniently packaged, the developments involved extend over three or four centuries, with different specific chronologies in each region.

The length of the classical period is also a challenge. Separate sub-periods may be identified for each region, depending on the amount of time available for detail. The movement from Zhou to Han dynasty, and related institutional and cultural change, is hardly a simple progression; Indian history is marked by several separate intervals, including the Mauryan and then, later, the Gupta dynasties; the distinctive Persian dynamic has already been noted. In the Mediterranean, the passage from Greece through Hellenism to Rome involves significant shifts in geographical base and focus, as well as important changes in characteristics. In strictly Western history this long period is conventionally broken up into the two or three chunks (Greece, Rome, and sometimes a separate inter-mediate pause for Hellenism), but most world historians shy away from this level of detailed treatment. Nevertheless, the challenge of internal change during the period is quite real, and not just for the Mediterranean.

POST-CLASSICAL

Coherence arguably improves in the post-classical centuries, despite the expansion in the number and range of societies to be covered. It's still true that key parts of the world are not embraced by the themes of the post-classical era, but the expansion of the civilization form in northern Europe, Africa, Southeast Asia and Japan reduces the scope of this problem. A bit of debate attends the date chosen to launch the period. Some world histories start the period up in 500, to capture developments in China, Western Europe and the Byzantine Empire, including the expansion of Buddhism and Christianity, while others urge 600 and the rise of Islam, which undeniably becomes a central theme. There's far more transitional complexity at the end of the period, once Arab preeminence begins to yield and the new roles for China, the Mongol period, and innovations in Western Europe must be taken into account. Finally, some world historians urge a division of the post-classical period, around 1000 CE, mainly to capture the importance of the patterns of trans-regional exchange that were in full operation by this point. The lack of convenient political definitions for the post-classical period overall, despite important political changes in individual societies, might be seen as an analytical trouble spot as well.

The issues of the post-classical period do not overshadow the fact that the period can be defined by major themes, which in turn differ from the major themes of the classical period and from which the themes of the early modern period (though linked to post-classical developments) will differ in turn. The ability to use changing regional dynamisms and power relationships and above all shifts in exchange patterns as core elements in periodization discussions shines through clearly.

EARLY MODERN

The greatest conventional challenge of the early modern period is the fact that it corresponds so closely with standard periodization in Western history, capturing the full flowering of the Renaissance and running through the Enlightenment, which deepens the danger of seeing the period excessively in Western terms. The challenge can be met, but it requires explicit effort. Some world historians have been concerned about the convenience date 1450 as the period's launch, arguing that the early 1500s would be better in highlighting the facts that the inclusion of the Americas was underway and that the importance of the Ottoman Empire was confirmed and extended by a victory over an Egyptian army (defeat of the Mamluks, 1517). Chinese historians have long pointed out that the 1450 date doesn't coincide with Chinese periodization, which more commonly would look to the establishment of the new Ming dynasty in the later fourteenth century. But while this kind of messiness can be noted — specific regional dynamics routinely differ from world history periodization choices — it hardly requires a different choice of date. Indeed, the Chinese decision in 1439 to halt its great trading expeditions adds to the importance of the mid-fifteenth century as the beginning of a major new world history transition which would include novel Western, Russian, and Ottoman activities as well.

Recently, a social scientist/historian, Jack Goldstone, has raised a new kind of issue about the early modern period. He sees these centuries as the beginning of the end for pre-modern, or agricultural patterns. Goldstone even wonders if world history periodization as a whole could be rethought: a new and longer ancient or pre-modern period would capture the heart of the agricultural experience, from the early civilizations in 3500 BCE onward to the end of the post-classical period. Then the next chunk of time, from the end of the post-classical all the way to 1900, would be grouped as the "late pre-modern." Obviously this alternative is partly a matter of labeling. But it also urges attention to the centuries after 1400, and not only in the West, as the seedbed for tentative innovations that would ultimately overturn the long-established agricultural patterns in politics and culture as well as the economy.

The final analytical vulnerability for the early modern period (calling attention to the period's brevity and spilling over into definitions of the long nineteenth century) is the lack of any clear marker for the period's end. The Seven Years War (1756–63) rebalanced power relations in Europe, shifted British policies in North America and, above all, cleared the way for growing British control of India. It was a geographically extensive conflict that both revealed and promoted growing European world power. And sometime around 1750 (though the 1770s are probably a better choice) the first clear signs of British industrialization began a vital economic and social transition in Europe and the world. On the other hand, it wasn't until around 1840 that Europe's economic relationship with China really changed, to Chinese disadvantage. And there's the whole question of how to fit in the French, Haitian and American revolutions, and the Latin American struggles for independence. The fact is that choosing an end to the early modern period and defining when new themes begin to seize center stage – crucial for defining the long nineteenth century – is a work in progress. There's no bitter debate here, aside from Goldstone's interesting proposal, but it would be possible for argue for a somewhat different set of periodization choices.

LONG NINETEENTH CENTURY

To date, however, world historians are in the main fairly attached to defining a separate "long 19th century,", even though the period is quite short and even though many of the clearest new themes, including the full global impact of industrialization and the emergence of key characteristics of globalization, don't emerge clearly until the 1850s or so.

If major emphasis rests on Europe's growing world role and the related rise of settler societies like the United States, and the relative or absolute decline of most other areas, the long nineteenth century works well enough as a period, and the fact that it was a brief episode, with its end foreshadowed by the experiences and consequences of World War I, is part of the definition. This is a period shaped by power dynamics above all, and undone as the power dynamics began to change in the early twentieth century.

THE CONTEMPORARY ERA

The final potential world history period – the contemporary era still unfolding – inescapably involves different analytical issues from those surrounding other major periods because we don't know the end of the story. Definitions of new themes are inherently more tentative, and we will return to the question of the relationship between the contemporary world and world history in a final chapter.

Some world historians, facing the twentieth century and its particular complexities and uncertainties, simply accept a choppy periodization approach, noting the interwar decades as bookended by two major wars and embellished by the Depression, then turning to the Cold War and decolonization framework for the four decades after World War II, then talking about recent trends in a more open-ended fashion. Another group of historians, fascinated by the innovative force of globalization, downplay the first half of the twentieth century and see the 1950s as the turning point to the new era with globalization its organizing principle. There is, in sum, far less agreement about this most recent turn in world history periodization than about the issues involved in the earlier timeframes.

The key point, in this final exercise, is to know what the issues are in various options and, above all, to apply analytical criteria derived from earlier periodization assessments to the contemporary experience. The guidelines are clear: look for a reduction in the force of prior themes – most obviously, the themes of the long twentieth century – and simultaneously define new themes, including changes in power relationships and interaction patterns.

Periodization rests on decisions students and scholars make about how best to define time, and change within time. As with any set of decisions, alternatives can and should be discussed. Even if conventional decisions – as set forth, for example, in standard world history textbooks – seem fully acceptable, they must be examined, their bases understood. The result will spill over directly into the nurturance of appropriate habits of mind, and it will make the task of assimilating world history data – the factual materials – not only more meaningful but ultimately, by providing key highlights in advance, easier as well.

But decisions about time are only a first step in the process of understanding how world history is put together. They lead inescapably to the need for decisions about place. Basic world history periods set forth core themes, including changes in patterns of interaction, and by definition the themes must apply to a number of different societies. The themes do not, however, predict how the societies involved will handle the changes involved. The themes, in essence, are the global part of the world history exercise; they must be combined with the local and regional. Deciding about place – about how to define and handle different regional units – is the next step in the larger exercise.

FURTHER READING

Periodization is not discussed as often as might be imagined, given its centrality to historical research and teaching, but there are some important books and articles. See Lawrence Besserman, ed., *The Challenge of Periodization: Old Paradigms and New Perspectives* (New York: Routledge, 1996) and Jerry H. Bentley, "Cross-Cultural Interaction and Periodization in World History," in *American Historical Review* (June 1996): 749–70. See also Ross Dunn, "Periodization and Chronological Coverage in a World History Survey," in *What Americans Should Know: Western Civilization or World History?* Ed., Josef W. Konvitz (East Lansing: Michigan State University, 1985); and Jack Goldstone, "The Problem of the 'Early Modern' World," in *Journal of the Economic and Social History of the Orient* 41 (1998): 249–84. On Big History, see David Christian, *Maps of Time: An Introduction to Big History* (Berkeley: University of California Press, 2004).

5

MANAGING SPACE
WORLD HISTORY REGIONS AND CIVILIZATIONS

Turkey is a country largely located in southwestern Asia, but with a tip extending into southeastern Europe. The country has sometimes been controlled by Europeans, but prior to current nationhood was part of an Ottoman Empire that included both European and southwest Asian territory, and even a bit of North Africa. Turkey is predominantly Muslim but has been governed by a mostly secular government for over 80 years, during which time it sought to imitate Western patterns in many respects – including adopting a Western alphabet for its distinctive language (which is, however, related to Finnish, thanks to earlier Turkic migrations). Its dominant ethnicity as well as language differs from those of Arab and other neighbors on the Asian side. Turkey recently applied for membership in the European Union, and has adopted further contemporary Western patterns – including abolition of the death penalty – as part of this process. The application has stalled, however, with various European leaders indicating their belief that Turkey is too different from Europe to be included. So where is Turkey? What region is it part of? Is it a section of Asia (which is where it mostly is geographically)? Or Europe (where some of its leaders seem to want to be, at least economically and politically)? Or must it simply be regarded as a special case, a region unto itself, and if so how many special mid-sized regions of this sort must be identified within a world history program?

The Turkish example is just one of the many dilemmas involved in picking regions for treatment in world history. It slightly straddles geographic regions; its history suggests a changing regional identity depending on cultural and political factors; its own sense of regional identity may differ from the identity some of its neighbors (particularly, now, its European neighbors) assign to it.

Places, in world history, are determined by a combination of geographical features and shared historical experiences. Geography is crucial, and world history depends on some knowledge not just of where things are but of physical features and boundaries, including climate zones. But geography does not alone determine what regions cohere and what regions differentiate. Shared cultures and institutions are also vital. This chapter deals with the issues involved with identifying regions and the related question of defining civilizations. Place, in world history, sometimes corresponds with political boundaries, but this is not always – indeed, not usually – the case. Many students, trained in their own national history, assume that nations are the logical unit of analysis. Happily (since there are now over 200 independent states) this is not true, and many crucial and definable regions characteristically operate amid political divisions and even a great deal of internal warfare (neighborhood belligerence can after all be a shared regional characteristic).The result is that places have to be decided upon – they do not drop magically from a world atlas or from a list of current membership in the United Nations. Decisions, in turn, combine analytical components – about shared geography and history – with practical considerations, involving how much time is available for finer-grained regional details. The mixture, of the analytical and the pragmatic, duplicates for space the same basic set of considerations relevant to periodization.

DEBATES ABOUT GEOGRAPHICAL SCOPE

Decisions about place may generate more dispute in and around world history than periodization does. Historians are mostly trained to be very place-specific. They're experts on Korea or France or Brazil, sometimes prodded into teaching a slightly wider course on East Asia or Europe or Latin America but not keen on diluting their very substantial knowledge of local detail with too much regional generalization. Currently, in the historical profession as a whole at least in the United States, regional specializations are becoming if anything fiercer (despite the rise of world history), as scholars eagerly participate in meetings and exchange publications with other experts on their particular area. There is even a group of micro-historians who argue that any place larger than a small locality generates an unacceptable level of oversimplification and inaccuracy.

Because world history decisions about place cannot fully overlap with regional criteria in more specialized fields – European historians, for example, easily recognize the special place of France, but world historians don't usually have time to explore how France differs from other parts of Western Europe – a certain amount of analytical tension is inevitable. One of the most successful recent ventures in world history, at least in terms of wide public notice, a 1997 book by Jared Diamond, involved an effort not only to deal with very big regions, but to argue that the particular geographies of these big regions have deeply affected, possibly determined, human history from early days on to the present. Diamond was fundamentally interested in explaining why clearly intelligent, hardworking people in some societies found it so difficult to achieve levels of power and prosperity available in other regions. Rejecting genetic explanations that might argue that some races are superior to others biologically, Diamond found the basic answer in regional geographic distinctions. The big gap, to his mind, was between Eurasia (embracing societies like China, India, Russia and Western Europe) and the rest of the world, but most particularly places like Africa and the native societies of the Americas and Australia. Without much question, some of the largest and most successful civilizations in world history developed in Asia or Europe and with no question at all some of them, particularly from Europe, conquered or displaced peoples in a number of regions outside the Eurasian landmass.

The causes of this basic regional divide, Diamond argues, lay in the disparity between the plants and animals available in Eurasia, compared to those elsewhere. Beginning with the rise of agriculture in southwest Asia, Eurasians had access to an unusual range of productive crops, such as wheat and barley, which are high in nutrients and can be easily planted. In contrast, Native Americans had to rely on corn, where planting is much more laborious and which has fewer nutrients, making it more difficult to develop surpluses. The animal gap was if anything even greater. Eurasians could call on some of the most useful and docile animals to be found anywhere, such as donkeys, bullocks, cows, pigs and chickens. Africans had largely wild animals to contend with, and while they could import Eurasian animals, disease problems, particularly those caused by the tse tse fly, made local breeding difficult. Americans had virtually no useful animals at all, and Australians effectively had none until species were brought in from Eurasia. Finally, Eurasians benefited from a roughly shared climate that made it relatively easy to spread crops and animals from one place to another along east-west routes. Again in contrast, in the Americas, potential transmission routes ran mainly north-south, but this involved huge differentiations in climate that made it very difficult to use crops developed in one place, like corn, nearly as widely.

Few world historians fully accept Diamond's approach to regionalization. They would note the importance of more regionally precise cultural patterns, as against fairly barebones geographic determinism. At the same time, elements of the shaping power of geography over distinctive regional patterns are inescapable, and the approach can obviously be expanded. India, reachable overland through several mountain passes and of course at many points by sea, proved historically more open to contacts than China, though it is vital to note that China too was not completely closed off. China, as a society, benefited from a highly productive agriculture in part because fertile top soils from central Asia regularly blow in thanks to prevailing winds, giving the nation a natural economic advantage over its western neighbors that shows up still today. The role of climate in Russian history is obvious, until recently requiring an unusually large percentage of people to work the land in comparison with those available for urban occupations and inspiring many military and diplomatic efforts to gain access to warm water ports. There is no doubt that a variety of geographic factors help define distinct regional experiences, though arguably the technologies and communications possible over the past 200 years will gradually modify, or potentially modify, some of the gaps.

REGIONAL CHOICES

The kind of regional issues that preoccupy most world historians pull away from the extremes of localism on the one hand, or sweeping geographic determinism on the other. Some of the issues revolve very simply around the question of how many regions it's practical to identify, and here the number partly depends on how much time for detail a world history program has. Other issues highlight the fact that some regions are harder to agree upon than others, for a mixture of geographic and historical reasons.

Here, quite simply, is a current list of "regions that must be known," from one major world history program (the Advanced Placement course). It leads immediately to a discussion of how and why some regions are clearer than others (and also, what's left out even from this worthy effort). The list: North Africa, West Africa, East Africa, Equatorial Africa, Southern Africa, Middle East, East Asia, Southeast Asia, Latin America and South Asia. At least three regions – Eastern and Western Europe and Central Asia – are not included because they constitute cultural areas that "have changed often over time."

Several of the entrants seem pretty clear. East Asia is a term often used in world history, to embrace China, most obviously, but also Korea and Japan, both nearby and often influenced by China, and usually Vietnam as well.

South Asia is another fairly clear case, neatly framed geographically by the Indian subcontinent, though usually embracing Sri Lanka. The Advanced Placement map, however, includes the largely Muslim nation of Bangladesh as part of the region (most of which is taken up by India), but pushes Pakistan and Afghanistan (two other Muslim cases) into the Middle East, which is actually questionable except in terms of shared religious affiliation.

The Middle East (more accurately but less commonly referred to as southwest Asia), though often (as at present) divided into different political units, has a measure of regional coherence. The eastern boundaries have varied, as already noted: Persia and Alexander the Great's empire extended into Afghanistan and Pakistan, but these areas, or parts of them, often figure in the South Asian story instead. The Caspian and Black Seas provide a reasonably clear northern border to the Middle East, as does the Mediterranean to the west and Indian Ocean to the south. Separation from North Africa, however, is less clear-cut, as the Red Sea does not run all the way to the Mediterranean, and culturally and sometimes politically North Africa and the Middle East have been joined.

Other sections are regionally harder to define. Southeast Asia is, obviously, east of South Asia and south of East Asia, which helps a bit. It would always include the current nations of Myanmar, Thailand and Malaysia, and normally covers the vast island territories of Indonesia as well. But should the Philippines be included in Southeast Asia, despite a somewhat separate island location and a considerably different historical experience? The fact that Southeast Asia is, and has been, disunited both politically and culturally combines with less clear geographical boundaries to make a more complex regional case.

Central Asia is a puzzle because it has so rarely been the center of organized states, but rather a mixture of nomadic territories combined more recently with encroachments from neighboring empires – like the Chinese, Russian or Ottoman. With the fall of the Soviet Union the region is now dominated by separate nations, both west but particularly east of the Caspian Sea. But China's western area impinges on central Asia (which might otherwise be seen as extending to Mongolia), and Russia still controls largely Islamic regions – some of them, like Chechnya, quite restive – that also fall within the region.

Africa, in the presentation suggested above, clearly poses some interesting regional challenges. This is the second largest continent, after Asia, so considerable regional diversity is hardly surprising. But there is no clear agreement, at the world history level, about how to handle the result. We will see that generalizations do not always honor the relatively detailed regional scheme suggested in the Advanced Placement world history course.

It is not hard to identify *North Africa*. The region, separated from most of the rest of Africa by the great Sahara desert, has both a distinct geography and a distinct history, often linked either to other parts of the Mediterranean or to the Middle East or both.

Division of the remainder of Africa into four major chunks corresponds, as usual, to a mixture of geographical features and historical experiences. *East Africa*, reaching in from the Indian Ocean coast but also including the islands of Zanzibar and Madagascar, has never been a political unit. *Southern Africa* was settled later than most other regions on the continent, with farming and iron-using groups well established by 500 BCE but with pockets of hunter–gatherers operating as well. *West Central Africa*, stretching northward from the southern region but largely away from the Atlantic coast, features more highly forested areas. This region includes much of the

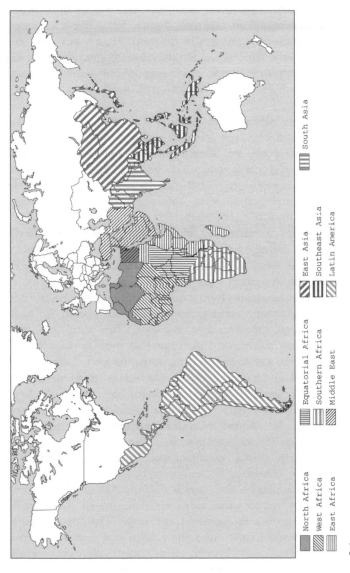

Figure 5.1

Congo basin, but also the eastern part of present-day Nigeria and stretching on up toward the Sahara. Finally, *West Africa*, also below the Sahara but closer to the Atlantic coast, was often referred to as the Sudanic region in the post-classical period (even though the modern nation of Sudan lies to the east). Here was where some of the great early African kingdoms arose, beginning with Ghana, based in part on the region's extensive involvement in trans-Sahara trade, using both camels and horses introduced to the area from other places.

Regions in Africa can be fairly well defined. The obvious question for world history is whether the regions must be adopted as separate frameworks or if some larger overriding African features at all simplify the regional definitions. Here, opinions vary, and as always the issue combines pragmatic considerations – the more learning time, the more regional detail and accuracy can be ventured – with inescapable distinctions of place.

Latin America, embracing all of South America but also Central America including Mexico and the Caribbean, is the final region specifically outlined in the Advanced Placement course. The idea of a large Latin American region depends on the importance of the Spanish-Portuguese invasion and the subsequent colonial experience, which among other things established Spanish (or in Brazil, Portuguese) as the dominant language. This said, there are also important internal regional divisions that must be kept in mind in exploring this vast area, creating some tensions between general features and geographic specifics not totally different from those involved in Africa. The Andean region of the South American continent, for example, has a distinctive historical experience and also a large admixture of Native Americans and mestizos, in addition to its mountainous terrain, in contrast to the more temperate areas, with a greater population of European origin, such as Argentina or Uruguay.

This leaves, finally, the regions that the Advanced Placement list either ignores or views as unusually complicated – besides central Asia. There is, first, the question of Europe. The continent is joined to Asia, and the separation at the eastern end – mainly focused on the Ural Mountains in Russia – is not always clear cut. Distinctions between southern and northern Europe sometimes win attention: southern Europe shares many Mediterranean features with the western Middle East and North Africa, including relatively large villages, and direct exposure to the cultures and empires of classical Greece and Rome. But the big question, duly recorded in the Advanced Placement footnotes, involves east and west. Here, there is neither a clear nor a constant dividing line, though a few river systems, like the Elbe, may help a bit. The fact that Russia has long embraced considerable North Asian territory adds to the complexity.

The omissions from the Advanced Placement list raise their own issues. North America does not pose major identification problems, save for the common division between Mexico, as part of Latin America, and the rest of the continent. How to deal with Native American history in what is now the United States and Canada, however, is a regional issue most world historians so far largely evade.

Finally, there is the issue of Australia, New Zealand and the Pacific island chains. New Zealand, though relatively near, had a rather separate history from Australia until the past two centuries, as it was part of the great Polynesian expansion during the post-classical period that also reached places like Hawaii. The Pacific island chains themselves are relatively lightly populated and may receive relatively little attention at the world history level, save perhaps for brief mention of Western interest and occupation during the eighteenth to nineteenth centuries. Oceania is a challenging category.

SORTING OUT THE ROSTER

There are many regions in the world. Almost all of them require some decisions about internal coherence, external boundaries, and the overall combination of geographical markers and shared histories. Decisions about feasibility are also essential, and this will lead to disputes and differences in terms of the sheer number of regions identified.

Many regions have core societies, often fairly centrally located, and then other territories essentially in the same geographic neighborhood, where frequent interactions (both friendly and hostile) create a shared historical space. China's Middle Kingdom territory, defined by a mix of durable history and some geographic boundaries, thus links to the other parts of East Asia, with the main indeterminacies in the southeast (where there is no solid geographic line, and where China recurrently established frontier territories impinging into present day Vietnam) and in areas of periodic Chinese expansion in the west.

Regions can include some internally diverse geography, in terms both of climate and topography – the Indian subcontinent is a case in point, but so are north and south China and northern and southern Europe – so long as interactions and shared experience have at least partly cut across these features.

Other regions are defined more indirectly, and their clarity suffers in consequence. The various parts of Southeast Asia are close together, and many of them have recurrently interacted with each other, but they are marked also by NOT being part of China or India though open to influences from both. Central Asia similarly gains some shape through a combination of shared geography, but also its separation from powerful neighbors.

Many regions, understandably enough, have buffer zones, that sometimes seem best linked to territory in one direction, sometimes in another. The post-communist nations of east central Europe inhabit a territory that similarly can swing toward regions on either side, depending on historical circumstance; no definition-for-all time makes sense either historically or geographically.

Sub-Saharan Africa (leaving North Africa as a separate case) and Latin America (South and Central America plus the Caribbean) pose clear dilemmas of scale. Both can be defined in terms of large regions, with some broadly shared historical experiences at least at certain points in time, and obviously shared core continental geography (combined with some neighboring island groups). Both, however, have important internal regional distinctions in terms of topography, climate and history. Most world histories embrace the regions as a whole – for pragmatic reasons, in terms of time available, but also because of the possibility of identifying some cross-cutting factors (including colonialism, in recent centuries). But awareness of internal regional distinctions is also vital, to prevent misleading over generalization, particularly in the case of sub-Saharan Africa. There is no tidy formula.

Any regions list – whether as short as possible, slightly more detailed as with the Advanced Placement scheme, or more detailed still as in doing further justice to Latin America – risks seeming lifeless and even somewhat random. World historians would argue that a basic knowledge of regionalization is essential for the larger enterprise. This would include a shortlist of the indispensable regions and where they sit and how they are defined geographically, plus awareness of the arguments for a more detailed differentiation and the identification of cases (like Europe) that seem to raise particular definitional challenges. But world historians would also argue that this initial regional effort is only a first step, that more needs to be done to flesh out cultural and historical features that bring this geography into more vivid focus. One vehicle for this further discussion − overlapping with regionalization, but bringing in a larger historical component − involves using the civilization concept and the definitions and challenges that emerge from this.

CIVILIZATIONS AND REGIONS

Defining major civilizations is the crucial move in deciding on how to divide and categorize the world's regions in many world history programs. The concept of civilization combines the standard geographic features of many regions with a more historically informed sense of how particular areas have shared in political, economic and cultural experiences. It can also involve an active sense of identity, going beyond mere regional coexistence.

Civilization has several meanings, as we have seen, and they slide into each other in confusing fashion. Two of the meanings are useful in world history, and the third is decidedly not − but hard to get rid of. Civilization is first and foremost that complex form of human organization that initially emerged in Mesopotamia around 3500 BCE and involved organized states, some kind of urban network with related trade levels, and usually writing as a means of record-keeping and communication. Civilization also designates a broadly coherent set of cultural values and historical experiences that provide definable characteristics and often some sense of identity and continuity: this is the use of the civilization concept that looms largest in what follows. Indian civilization, in other words, involves both a recognition that India gained formal states, writing and the like, *and* a determination that the particular Indian version of civilization involves some characteristics specific to the subcontinent. Finally, however, there's a third meaning: the term civilization, or at least civilized, can point to superior kinds of behavior − more sophisticated tastes, better habits, less crudeness. This is a perfectly good definition, but it is really not useful in world history. The problem is that many civilizations do not predictably generate more of this behavior than other, non-civilizations do. People in civilizations can be more brutal and crude than those in many other types of societies. We will return to this problem after we explore the more useful definitions.

USING THE CIVILIZATION CONCEPT

The huge plusses in using civilizations as a regional and historical organizing principle are, first, that the number of core civilizations can be plausibly limited – ultimately, possibly to as few as seven or eight basic cases. This suggests, obviously, that certain civilizations extend beyond individual regions, which must be demonstrated but which is at least a defendable proposition. Australia and much of North America, for example, in this formulation ultimately become part of Western civilization, thanks to the expansion of pre-dominantly European populations, values and institutions. Of course they offer some special features, partly because of geography, partly because of population mix, but their inclusion in an expanded Western orbit at least serves as the basis for coherent analysis and discussion. Similarly, earlier on, thanks to the expansion of Islam and Arab culture and institutions, North Africa and the Middle East can be assessed in terms of participation in a single civilization, even though, during the early civilization period many centuries before, the political and cultural separation between Egypt and Mesopotamia required two distinct statements.

Besides potentially limiting the number of basic cases, we have seen that the civilization concept provides vital service in assessing limits on change. China, thus, though not unchanging, maintains certain aspects of identity from the classical period even to the present day, which helps define it as a civilization but also helps modify any impulse to overemphasize change or to unduly homogenize reactions to key forces like religious conversion or innovations in trans-regional trading networks.

Civilization, in sum, helps world historians deal both with issues of regional diversity and with change over time. Civilizations set fundamental categories for comparative analysis (in which, however, unexpected similarities must be noted along with the more familiar emphasis on differentiations). Not surprisingly, then, the civilization concept crops up in many world history projects, which is why sketching the most common formulations is a vital building block in establishing the basics of the whole field.

CAUTIONS AND CONCERNS

A few basic cautions attach to the use of civilization, aside from the importance of making sure a civilizational framework does not take over the whole world history presentation. Civilizations themselves must not be seen as entirely differentiated, for the very process of reacting to shared exchanges and even creating integrating institutions and values generated a surprising range of common features, which comparison must identify along with differences. And civilizations are not constants: not only do they change, but they sometimes disappear outright. The roster of civilizations that can be identified today is not the same as that of earlier periods. Mergers and new entrants spice the civilization panorama as well, ever since civilization as a phenomenon first emerged about 5500 years ago. Deciding to use civilization is only the first step: one must then proceed to the challenging task of deciding what civilizations, at any given time, best explain how key regions were structured.

There are two other preliminary issues – as always, both conceptual and practical – that can be identified before a more precise process of definition begins. All civilizations balance core features with several types of internal differences and disputes, and it's not always easy to strike a balance between the more obvious general aspects and some of the less uniform realities. It's sometimes tempting to present civilizations as uniform, tidy entities – but they never are. And second, all civilizations involve some particular tensions in dealing with change over time, and these must also be built into the overall approach to the whole civilizational phenomenon.

Demonstrating that a civilization shares certain internal characteristics is crucial to using civilizations as active components of world history presentations and as guides to regional definitions. But any civilization, and particularly a large one, will also incorporate a number of variants, based among other things on geography and politics. For post-classical Western Europe, for example, it's valid to point to an overall civilization based on shared Catholicism and political and economic forms like feudalism and manorialism. But France, gradually forming a feudal monarchy, and Germany, more divided internally within the loose Holy Roman Empire, were hardly the same, either politically or culturally, and they developed different specific languages. They also recurrently fought each other directly (though this also means they shared considerable warlike propensities – civilizations do not necessarily depend on internal harmony). Regional complexities apply even where there are no formal internal political boundaries. China can often seem to be a highly centralized civilization, and it often aspired to be: but south China embraces diverse languages and population groups compared to the north, quite apart from outright frontier regions in the west or southeast. Civilizations must be understood as providing some overarching characteristics which do not, however, define each internal region uniformly.

Civilizations also include different social groups, and these may participate more or less fully in some of the defining overall characteristics. Confucianism, for instance, marked Chinese culture and politics from the classical period onward. But particularly in the early phases Confucianism was much more fully integrated by the upper classes, especially the famous scholar gentry who staffed the bureaucracy, than by common folk. Ordinary people picked up elements of Confucianism – and arguably, for a civilization to hold together, there must ultimately be some cultural sharing among different social segments. Never, however, did full uniformity emerge.

Defining a civilization assumes that several core features and shared experiences did unite a region – sometimes, as with China or India, a large region – at least to some degree. These qualities are arguably more important, particularly at the world history level, than the regional and social divides and the internal differences and variants. Using defined civilizations is nevertheless a bit of a compromise, even in the most clear cut cases like China, as against a number of more fine-grained options. Exactly how the compromise is shaped depends in part, on the time available for detail, though the generalizations should never be allowed to oversimplify unduly.

The danger of overdoing continuity within civilizations captures the final general problem within the civilizational approach, though it is probably easier to deal with than with the challenge of striking the balance between the general and the divisive. Here's the issue:

defining a civilization makes it essential to show that some features last over time – unless the civilization, as an entity, disappears almost entirely, which does happen (witness ancient Egypt, or Byzantine civilization). If there's not some continuity, and the civilization changes stripes entirely with each passing period, it's hard to argue that the civilization really exists at all. But civilizations are not and can not be stagnant. They all must balance important changes against some durable characteristics. So the analytical use of civilization, over time, must capture this tension as well.

The precise nature of this problem varies with the case. China established successful traditions fairly early on, and we have seen that some scholars argue that it was particularly immune from challenge by frequent invasion (though breakdowns did occur). It can be tempting to see Chinese qualities as virtual constants, at least until the past century or two. But China did change while retaining key features from the past, in part because of shifts in patterns of contact, and it's essential to capture the interaction between change and continuity. In other instances – Western civilization may be a case in point – openness to change may be seen as a dominant feature, which makes it more difficult to determine what qualities, if any, really define the civilization over time. Here, then, it is vital to counter too much fascination with how much the West could shake off past systems by noting at least a few features that, from one period to the next, still made the West a common civilization in more than geographic terms. No civilization escapes the need to capture a mixture of continuity and change.

THE ROSTER OF CIVILIZATIONS: FORMATIVE TRADITIONS

While analysis of individual river-valley societies is valuable, it was in the classical period that reasonably durable civilizations began to emerge. That is, after all, why the term "classical" is used, in indicating societies that generated surviving legacies. The classical civilizations built on achievements from their river-valley predecessors. Greece and Persia thus turned to the heritage of Mesopotamian societies, and also Egypt; classical China used precedents from earlier Hwang Ho dynasties. But only in the classical period is it possible to say both that key regions began to share certain cultural, institutional and social characteristics AND that some of these features would last a long time – well after a single period was over.

This in turn is what defining a civilization requires, when the goal is not just to identify apparatus such as a formal state or some urban network but also to suggest what elements held a particular civilization together, usually over a considerable region, and differentiated it in some ways from other civilizations. For at least two of the classical civilizations, China and India, provide a real model for the criteria involved both in defining and utilizing a civilizational approach – and the fact that they were quite different, one from the other, reminds us that emphases that provide a civilization's coherence can vary considerably, from the heavily political, in the Chinese case, to the cultural-social, in that of India.

Here, using the Chinese and Indian examples, is what to look for: civilizations generate some characteristic cultural features, in these cases through major philosophies and religions that not only spread widely but helped shape political and social institutions. Shared culture was augmented by some shared institutional experience (particularly vivid in the Chinese case) and/or characteristic social structures (particularly striking in the Indian case). These shared features – cutting across more than one aspect of the society's activity – both reflected and promoted common historical experiences from the classical period onward, and they operated within contiguous regions that can be to some extent identified geographically. Finally, the features, though open to various kinds of innovation including shifts that resulted from new external influences, demonstrate considerable durability. No one should confuse contemporary China or India with their classical predecessors, for a multitude of changes have intervened: but India is still powerfully shaped by Hinduism and grapples still with legacies of the caste system, while China retains, in sharply modified forms, several remnants of a Confucian legacy.

As Islamic civilization formed under Arab leadership in the Middle East and North Africa, another fairly clear civilization category emerged. Islamic culture provided the most obvious guiding force, but Arab political experience and social categories counted as well, along with some secular cultural forms. The civilization obviously built on earlier developments in the region, from the river-valley achievements through the Roman Empire, but its full expression awaited the post-classical period. Islam spread beyond this civilization region, and would play a role in India, Southeast and central Asia and Africa, but without enough shared political and social experience to form a definable civilization throughout the vast whole Islamic world. Even in the Middle East, the existence of a separate Persian tradition, along with various political divisions, periodically complicates the definition. But the basic criteria of definable features, beyond culture alone, and shared historical experience and geographical proximity, are easily met, along with the civilization's durability across time.

CIVILIZATIONS CHECKLIST

(1) What are the main characteristics of the civilization, in terms of identifiable cultural, political and social features?
(2) Is there a shared historical experience, and when did it begin?
(3) What features can be traced over time, however modified by change? Do these features continue in the present day?

Additional Issues

(1) What are the main complexities in defining the civilization, in terms of internal regional or social tensions?
(2) Did the civilization interact with or imitate other societies, and did this affect any major characteristics?
(3) What have been the main changes to the definition of the civilization over time?

WESTERN CIVILIZATION

A fourth clear tradition is usually identified in world history, as it developed in Western Europe. There are a few twists to this case however, beginning with the need to avoid assumptions about special Western importance or superiority. The key issue involves discussing when and on what basis Western characteristics began to emerge – and what they are. Some features ultimately associated with the West developed in classical Greece and Rome – but the classical legacy also deeply affected the Middle East and also Eastern

Europe, while it was greatly modified in the West itself. There is no easy Greco-Roman/Western equation. Clearer Western features took shape during the post-classical centuries, including the Western version of Christian culture and politics, and some other widespread political and social forms (including the surprisingly pervasive internal warfare). But the West would change considerably in the early modern centuries, particularly with the new importance of science in the overall cultural mix. Some observers have argued that an identifiable Western characteristic is the unusual ability to change, but this claim needs careful comparison with the flexibility of other regions (for example, Japan). Western civilization, as a concept, is used as a label more commonly than as an analytical category, for identifying its characteristics requires care. Contemporary Western features, like political democracy, are often pushed farther back in the past than the evidence supports – again a sign that the West, while usable as a civilizational category, needs some critical evaluation, and careful comparison, as it is explored in the world history project.

The fact is that identifying civilizations – as coherent frameworks for important aspects of the human experience – is easier in some cases than others, because of the different ways regional histories unfolded. This does not mean that some civilizations are better than others. It does mean that while there are some very general basic criteria for defining a civilization, in terms of shared experiences and durability, the phenomenon also has to be approached to some extent on a case by case basis. Different kinds of complexities apply, as the Western evolution already suggests.

AFRICA

Developments in Africa are extremely important in world history from the river-valley period onward – quite apart from the vital earlier fact that the species originated there. But there is no question that pulling Africa into the civilizational framework involves some special challenges. Many world histories refer to sub-Saharan African civilization, but there are several problems in this formulation that differ from what we've encountered so far in exploring the civilizational category.

The first problem is more apparent than real, but it may still affect perceptions because of longstanding misconceptions about

African history and the undeniable difficulties many contemporary African nations face today. Western observers long assumed that Africa was uncivilized, at least until the arrival of Europeans began to introduce more elevated standards. This is historical nonsense. Civilization as a form of human organization began in sub-Saharan Africa quite early, initially in the Upper Nile region with Kush and its successors. By the post-classical period organized states and urban networks were spread more widely, though admittedly not through the whole vast subcontinent. Indeed, even in the early modern period direct European penetration of most of West Africa was limited by the strength of existing states. It is also true that contemporary Africa includes some very poor regions and also that levels of political turmoil have been high, but these facts carry no particular retrospective message except to invite comparison with periods of political turmoil in the experience of other societies.

The regional subdivisions of Africa pose an obvious challenge, though few argue for separate regional civilizations here. Further, enough crosscurrents involve different regions – the range of the Bantu migrations and the related extensive spread of Bantu languages and cultures, the impact of Islam (far greater, admittedly, in some regions than others), and then the impact of European imperialism and decolonization – to permit discussions of shared experiences.

The final issue involves the fact that Africa, while generating important local cultures, has also imported a number of great traditions from other societies – such as Islam, Christianity, even nationalism. Africans have adapted these traditions creatively, not merely copying, and they have often combined them in distinctive ways. But there is not the clear-cut African cultural monument to point to as there is for China and the West. This is true in many other cases – Africa is not at all unique here – but it is a further complexity particularly in combination with the other concerns.

SOUTHEAST ASIA

Southeast Asia poses some challenges similar to those of Africa, though it is fair to say that most world historians have grappled with them less extensively. The region developed civilization as a form of human organization early, in some cases during the classical period, quite widely by the post-classical. But the region's coherence was somewhat constrained by the diverse geography. Certainly there was never a period of even fleeting political unity or (at least until a common encounter with Western imperialism by the nineteenth century) a full sharing of historical experience aside from widespread participation in Indian Ocean trade.

As with Africa, furthermore, Southeast Asia was more a recipient than a generator of striking cultural movements. Regional cultural practices abound, in many cases much-studied by eager anthropologists. But the more unifying cultural and historical experiences resulted from extensive imports from India (including Hinduism and even more widely Buddhism), China (including important Chinese merchant minorities in many parts of the region), and the Middle East (Islam). Partly because of extensive borrowings, partly because of shared experiences in Indian Ocean trade and with British and Dutch colonialism, partly because of limits on the time available for detail in world history surveys, some categorizations seek to lump Southeast Asia in a larger "South and Southeast Asia" category. Save as a matter of convenience, however, the linkage is questionable: India and Southeast Asia were civilizations in contact, but not a single civilization in definitional terms. Here is a world history work in progress.

EAST ASIA AND EASTERN EUROPE

Japan, Korea and Vietnam – in addition to China in the East Asia region – and Russia and parts of Eastern Europe also challenge the civilizational approach, but for different reasons. The question in these cases involves balancing extensive connections and overlap with a neighboring region with the existence of clearly independent qualities. At what point does substantial and deliberate imitation blur civilizational lines? These are cases in which judgment calls could go in either direction; there is no definitive answer. But the doubts and questions are themselves revealing, showing the utility of a civilizational approach in identifying issues, even among uncertainties and debates.

Japan, Korea and Vietnam were never part of a single political unit with China or (with the exception of Japanese occupation) with each other. All three areas, currently, feel a strong sense of separate regional or national identity, and hostilities within the region are often considerable. Yet the areas also experienced massive Chinese influence over long periods of time, from the late classical period onward. The result is a great deal of sharing in art, literary culture, religion, social outlook, and particularly Confucianism. To be sure, some Chinese staples did not gain entry, including Daoism in the cultural sphere, foot binding for women in the social sphere. And none of these areas precisely imitated Chinese politics, despite some periodic efforts to replicate a Chinese-type imperial structure.

So is it most useful to see a larger East Asian civilization zone, based on heavy Chinese influence but including regions each a bit different from the other? Or does accuracy compel at least a recognition of Japanese civilization, linked to but separate from the Chinese case? The debate is healthy, even if it cannot be fully resolved. And it's not just a historical issue. Many analysts have talked about the importance of modified Confucian values in shaping a distinctive, and obviously successful, approach to the challenge of industrialization in the contemporary world. Japan responded first here, but the economic surge of South Korea and now China may be evidence that the region shares more than might be imagined. The argument here is that East Asian patterns differ from those of the West, for example through the extensive involvement of the state in the economy; but also from other parts of the world that have not to date responded quite as vigorously to industrial opportunities. The idea of a larger civilization zone cannot be dismissed out of hand.

Russia is a clear challenge, as the regional discussion already indicated. It's fair to say that both European historians and world historians register some uncertainties here. Beginning with the European territories of the Byzantine Empire in the post-classical period, eastern as well as Western Europe became increasingly Christian. But the versions of Christianity, and its political and cultural implications, were rather different from east to west, making it difficult to cover both parts of Europe with the same civilization umbrella. After the collapse of the empire and with the subsequent rise of Russia, the question of civilization was reformulated. Russia and other parts of Eastern Europe (outside the Ottoman Empire in the southeast) interacted increasingly with the West. By the eighteenth and nineteenth centuries something of a common high culture emerged, with east European artists and writers contributing actively to a shared intellectual endeavor; and scientists joined in as well. But east European politics and key aspects of popular culture were rather different, and many of these differences, though redefined, continued into the twentieth century. A segment of Russian leadership also worried actively about too much identification with the West, preferring to stand by different Russian values. Finally, social structures differed even more substantially, at least until the late twentieth century, with a smaller urban segment and more large-estate agriculture in the eastern zone. Was Russia part of the West, with some clear differences, or do we need a separate category? Most world historians opt for the latter decision or simply downplay Russia and Eastern Europe altogether; but a more active debate may be desirable.

Some societies, in sum, and important ones at that, develop patterns of contact and imitation, without, however, entirely merging with the civilization with which they are interacting. Discussing definitions here may be frustratingly inconclusive, but they actually reveal important characteristics of all the parties involved. They don't produce a magically agreed-upon civilization map for world history, but they generate a sense of civilizational complexities that can advance understanding.

RECENT CIVILIZATIONS

By this point, it will not come as a surprise that serious definitional dilemmas apply to areas where the establishment of ongoing civilizations is more recent than in the case of Japan, Russia or Southeast Asia.

The Americas are a challenge to world historians in several ways – which is one reason why, until recently, the regions tended to be given short shrift in favor of Asia, Europe and usually Africa.

Challenge #1 simply involves deciding how to cover the Americas before 1492 – before, in other words, they were part of an ongoing set of global contacts. Two civilization areas emerged in the Americas, that certainly deserve attention – chronologically, in the classical and particularly post-classical periods. Important societies periodically developed in North America as well. But American patterns, while they can usefully be compared to early civilizations elsewhere – the Mayans with river-valley civilizations in Mesopotamia, the Incas with Egypt – did not follow the periodization dynamic applicable to Afro-Eurasia. To take a single example: the Mayan experience begins in the classical period but continues into the mid-post-classical, with some internal changes that have nothing to do with the period of classical decline in Afro-Eurasia. Omission of the Americas before European contact would improperly cut off an important dimension of the human story, quite apart from the additions to a comparative understanding of how early civilizations emerged and operated. Omission would also unfairly slight a set of patterns, particularly in central America and the Andes, that would have some impact on American developments even later on. But there is no way to make appropriate inclusion entirely smooth, because the essential element of world history periodization, involvement in a definable contact pattern, is simply missing. This also means that practical considerations, in terms of how much time is available for detail, weigh in as well.

The second challenge for the American experience, once European and African contacts become extensive from the sixteenth century onward, involves definitional issues that overlap with factors already considered in dealing with sub-Saharan Africa or Russia, though obviously with different specifics.

Latin American civilization is a category often employed, but it must be tested through two types of now-familiar questions. First, is the category coherent enough, in terms of shared cultures, institutions and historical experience, to stand up against clear internal regional differences of the sort discussed in the previous chapter? Most world histories use Latin America without too much apology, even trying to embrace the Caribbean, but current surveys of Latin American history by area specialists almost always subdivide by region. Some overall coherence is defendable, through attention to Spanish and Portuguese impacts, including Catholicism, and the emergence of an economy and related social structure based on production of foods and minerals for world trade. But, at the least, the tension with internal differentiations must be noted.

At the other extreme – and here the Russian example offers some interesting parallels, despite a very different specific history – Latin Americanists and world historians alike have debated whether Latin America is best regarded as a special case of a larger Western civilization, or whether it has to be understood as a separate category. By the sixteenth century, transportation improvements were beginning to make it possible to extend important aspects of one civilization – the West, in this case – to areas at a considerable distance. Latin America would share many aspects of Western high culture, in art and literature, and ultimately elements of Western political traditions, particularly in the emergence of liberalism from the early nineteenth century onward. Many Latin American elites would look to Europe as a model in other areas, in public hygiene, for example, or family or gender policy.

On the other hand, the influence of Native American and (in some areas) African populations and cultures may qualify a full sense of Latin America as a version of the West. Even more, the characteristic economic structure of Latin America, based on cheap labor and extensive importation of industrial goods, and resultant social divisions, argue for a separate civilizational category. As with Russia, high culture and popular experience did not point in the same directions, where relationships with Western civilization are concerned. As with Russia, either civilizational decision – whether Western or separate – requires some special explanation and qualification. The result hardly erases the capacity to add Latin America to the larger roster of civilizations – for a decision can be made and defended – but adds some unavoidable complexity.

AMERICAN EXCEPTIONALISM

Finally, there is the case of what many world historians call the settler societies of the early modern period and nineteenth centuries – Canada, New Zealand, Australia and above all (in terms of ultimate size and global influence) the United States. These were societies with substantial European immigration and influence, but also interactions with native populations and with a frontier experience that can be usefully compared with the Latin American story.

As world history was developing as a teaching field, particularly in the United States, there was a strong initial temptation not to do very much with the national history. After all, most students encountered United States history in other courses, and there was enough to cover without adding this in. This decision was untenable: it provided insufficient attention to a society that became a major force in world history at least by the later nineteenth century (with some influence earlier on), and it failed to provide an explicit world history framework for the national story itself.

But if the United States is to be included (along with some bows to the other settler societies), the familiar civilizational question arises: is this yet another case, or can it be seen as an extension of Western patterns? Good bits of American history, and some prestigious university programs, are organized around the idea that there is a distinct American civilization. An approach called *American exceptionalism* argues that while the United States was undoubtedly shaped by important European influences, by the early nineteenth century at least, a different kind of society was emerging (some would argue also, a better kind) that was an exception to European standards. Because of frontier experience and (some would argue) unusual material abundance, the mixing of races and ethnic groups, and the success of the American Revolution (among other things), the nation began developing differently, along its own special path.

On the other hand, the United States did maintain close contact with European patterns. It's hard to argue for a really separate United States literary or artistic culture, as opposed to participation in a larger Western or international movement. The United States industrialized along with Europe, it shifted to lower birth rates essentially along with Europe, it later committed (1950s–1960s) to new work roles for women along with Europe. There's a case to be made, as well, for the United States (and the other settler societies) as extensions of Western patterns with a few important adjustments.

CIVILIZATION AND CHANGE

There's a final twist to the definitional puzzle: the answers to questions about civilization definitions can change over time. Thanks to common economic and political patterns, for example, the United States and Western Europe became more similar in the decades after World War II – experiencing what some analysts call increasing convergence. By the end of the twentieth century, however, new differences emerged, as the United States became more defined by high levels of military commitment and also new surges of religious intensity, both of which Western Europe was largely casting off. Japan and China converged in many ways during the early modern period, as Confucianism gained greater influence in Japan, but then moved apart during the decades after 1868 when Japan committed to a reform movement and China headed toward revolution. Russia's modern relationship with the West, similarly, has not been constant.

Using civilizations to help organize world history is obviously not an exact science. Fairly clear-cut cases contrast with more ambiguous situations, and these latter do not always hold still over time. The complexities are not, however, impossible to handle. The effort to define the characteristics of a civilization leads to important comparative questions that can advance understanding of regional categories even when no definitive roster emerges.

DEBATING THE USES OF CIVILIZATIONS

Some world historians object to the use of the civilization concept because it can imply an invidious distinction between one group of societies and the many others that simply don't meet the definitional criteria of a civilization. Many civilizations often painted other groups as "barbarian," and more broadly it is hard to separate the idea of civilization from some idea of advancement. At the least, an unwarranted distinction between civilizations and "others" needs attention – including explicit treatment of nomadic and other cultures.

Use of civilization can also seem to divide attention into separate stories, whereas world history is meant to bring connections to the fore. Here's a second type of concern, though it can combine with the worries about invidious comparisons. One world historian, thus, has proposed the use of contact regions, like the Mediterranean or Indian Ocean basins, rather than civilizations, as a primary organizing principle. It is certainly true that some purported world history projects place so much emphasis on separate civilizations that the result is a sense of one set of experiences, then another, in a turgid kind of regional shopping list. There is no inherent reason, however, for the use of civilizations to degenerate into this one-thing-after-another pattern. Comparison is vital to make sense of individual civilizations, to highlight what is in fact distinctive about them and to encourage discussion of the causes of major differences as well as common qualities; this already cuts into a mechanical listing of civilizations. Equally important, civilizations must also be juxtaposed with whatever contact system operated at the time, and comparison can then highlight how one civilization's involvement lined up with other regions in terms of outreach and impact. Analyzing the interaction between a civilization and the changing patterns of trans-regional exchange is a vital component of the whole civilizational approach in world history.

Using civilizations is a choice. Over time, other approaches may gain further attention, as they reduce some of the baggage civilizations can involve. It is already true that world histories involve less focus on "major" civilizations, one after the other, and more attention to comparisons, contacts, and responses to common trans-regional forces than was the case just a decade or two ago. This is one of the key fruits of the maturation of the field, moving from a heavily area studies focus to a more global approach. Still, it is hard to avoid recognition that, in world history, the force of cultural and institutional experience did make Chinese reactions to global forces different from Indian or Arab – that, in other words, there were different civilizations at play. Human lives were shaped by the specific civilizational framework as well as the impact of larger contacts or transmissions. Opting for attention to civilizations needs some caution; it should never provide the exclusive analytical structure in world history. But it can be justified, and it can help organize some otherwise very difficult choices about regional variation and the ways in which global patterns are filtered by different traditions and trajectories.

FURTHER READING

A few outstanding efforts at regional categorization are available. See Fernand Braudel, *The Mediterranean and the Mediterranean World in the Age of Phillip II*, 2 vols. (Berkeley: University of California Press, 1996); Michael Pearson, *The Indian Ocean* (New York: Routledge, 2003); Douglas Egerton, et al., *The Atlantic World: A History, 1400–1888* (Wheeling, WV: Harlan Davidson, 2007); and Jared Diamond, *Guns, Germs and Steele: The Fates of Human Societies*, rev. ed. (New York: W.W. Norton & Company, 1999). On Africa, see J.D. Fage and W. Tordoff, *A History of Africa* (London: Routledge, 2002); and on Central Asia, see E. Allworth, ed., *Central Asia, 130 Years of Russian Dominance: a historical overview, 3rd ed.* (North Carolina: Duke University Press, 2002). On Oceania, refer to P. D'Arcy, *The People of the Sea: environment, identity and history in Oceania* (Honolulu: University of Hawaii Press, 2006). On Latin America, see Peter Bakewell, *A History of*

    Latin America: c. 1450 to the present (Oxford, UK: Blackwell Publishing, 2004); and on Southeast Asia, see Milton E. Osborne, *Southeast Asia: an introductory history* (Crows Nest, Australia: Allen & Unwin, 2005).

On civilizational issues: Charles C. Mann, *1491: New Revelations of the Americas Before Columbus* (New York: Vintage Books, 2006); and Carl Guarneri, *America in the World: United States History in Global Context* (New York: McGraw-Hill, 2007). See also John King Fairbank, *East Asia: Tradition and Transformation* (New York: Houghton Mifflin, 1997); and Merle Goldman and Leo Lee, eds., *An Intellectual History of Modern China* (United Kingdom: Cambridge University Press, 2002). See also Jerry H. Bentley's "Sea and Ocean Basins as Frameworks of Historical Analysis," in *Geographical Review* 89 (1999): 215–24; and *Seascapes: Maritime Histories, Littoral Cultures and Transoceanic Exchanges* (Honolulu: University of Hawaii Press, 2007).

6

CONTACTS AND THE STRUCTURE
OF WORLD HISTORY

Discussions of the main periods of world history, and the larger periodization frameworks, have already dealt with many aspects of the contacts that developed among various societies, at various points in time. Changes in contact patterns – especially though not exclusively through shifts in trade exchanges – are the single most important component in determining transitions from one major time period to another. It is clear that, whether using a civilizational approach or not, world historians have become increasingly fascinated by contacts and how much they add to our understanding of the human story. Contacts press beyond treating one civilization at a time, while also allowing for different reactions to interactions when they do occur.

Contacts can be double-edged, of course. They can spur mutual hostilities and violence. On the whole, however, contacts have helped the human species translate gains from one region to another – whether the focus involves different types of foods, new technologies, or new styles. They have stimulated change. And they have produced rich human stories, when individuals or groups encountered strange and wonderful behaviors in societies distant from their own.

World historians are interested in all sorts of human encounters. They develop case studies of interactions through migration, disease exchange, imperial expansion, long distance trade, missionary activity, or the diffusion of foods and technologies. They use changes in systems of encounters, including their base in transportation and communications technologies, as one of the organizing principles of the overall human story. They seek to balance attention on the formation of separate traditions – often, the emergence of durable civilizations – with the ways in which encounters prompt or force adjustments and innovations.

Many world historians are particularly eager to show that the obvious contemporary importance of encounters has a clear and steady historical backdrop. As one text puts it, "global interactions ... are by no means new features in world history." By showing how exchanges developed in earlier times, world history provides opportunities to demonstrate what's new but also to emphasize that the encounters of today fit into a larger continuum. There are indeed some patterns to encounters, some general features that do help an exploration of interactions whether the focus is on a long time ago or on tomorrow.

This chapter does not cover all major encounters. It shows why interactions and contacts are so fascinating. It shows how they often generate unexpected kinds of change. It discusses some general patterns in the results of interactions. There are no firm laws of history here, but there are some common responses that can help guide interpretations both for the past and for the present. Finally, the chapter returns to the question of change and continuity in the history of interregional contacts. The clear excitement about exploring early cases of contact – one of the real spurs to world history research over the past two decades – should not prevent us from asking also, how contacts have changed.

THE HUMAN SIDE

Ultimately, the real point of exploring contacts in world history involves determining how societies influence each other, the levels of significance of different forms of contact, and changes in systems of contact over time. But there's a less formal, often more personal aspect, that helps explain the fascination of contacts for many world historians and the considerable effort that has been devoted to discovering contact experiences even in relatively early phases of world history.

Initial ventures are of course wrapped up in considerable mystery. We know about the massive waves of early human migration out of Africa, including contacts among different species of humans at some points. But we have no way of knowing what the human experience was, what kinds of new learning or new resistance developed. It's also vital to remember that, until quite recently, few migrants ever returned to their place of origin, which limited the contact aspect of their travels.

Even as more organized societies emerged, we know little about the nature of interactions. Sea shells from the Indian Ocean were reaching Syria (on the Mediterranean coast of the Middle East) as early as 5000 BCE, which showed that trade had developed between the two regions. But how this affected those involved is anybody's guess.

Early contacts were also often constrained by the fact that they occurred in short hops, rather than directly bridging between major regions. By 2500 BCE Egypt was regularly trading for goods – mainly spices – from India. But the exchange went through centers in the Middle East, like the present-day nation of Bahrain (then called Dilmun): Egyptians and Indians undoubtedly had some contacts there, but an explicit Egypt to India link did not develop. We have seen (Chapter 2) that similar qualities described trade along the silk roads. Chinese goods reached the Middle East and the Mediterranean, but Chinese people did not, and there was scant mutual knowledge from one region to the next.

Contact was also impeded – and this is a theme that carries on right up to our own times – by mutual suspicions. Merchants were often distrusted, particularly if they were also foreigners. Classical Greeks relied heavily on merchants from the Middle East, but they did not grant them citizenship and they looked down on them in many ways. Many early societies used captured foreigners as slaves, yet another type of contact that might promote some wider learning about other ways of doing things; but slave status did not exactly encourage sweeping interactions.

At the same time, we know that contacts could also stimulate excitement as opportunities expanded. Urban crowds in Mesopotamia began enjoying exotic animals brought in from Africa: one poem wrote of "beasts from distant lands jostling in the great square," with reference to elephants and various apes. Consumer goods, like silks and spices, drew attention to the advantage of commercial contacts. By the third millennium BCE, clusters of foreign merchants located in cities across the Middle East, to facilitate trade with their homelands; in the process, they could bring awareness of other alternatives to local ways of doing things. By the classical period, a certain amount of tourism even developed, though mainly within major regions rather than from one area to the next. Wealthy Romans thus might go to see Greek and Egyptian monuments in the eastern Mediterranean. When governments like the Persian Empire began setting up road systems but also travelers' inns, they both reflected and encouraged additional kinds of contact.

A fascinating and almost inevitable aspect of contact involved the mixture of facts and fancy that encounters could generate, and here too there is some continuity between past and present though presumably we contemporaries are a bit less likely, with the abundant contacts available today, to invent outrageous stories about strange people. The Greek traveler Herodotus, in the fifth century, was eager to write about the places he visited and was deeply sympathetic to foreign cultures – even those of Greece's enemy Persia. But he also loved to describe peoples beyond his travels, whom the Greeks had only vaguely heard of, and he had little sense of what was implausible. He gave a stab at discussing the Indus River valley, noting correctly that people there wore cotton clothing; but he also claimed that men and women in the region engaged in sexual intercourse in public, "as herd animals do," and that they found gold in the desert after it was dug up by ants that were "bigger than foxes."

The late classical and post-classical periods expand the range of encounter stories available. By the time of the Han dynasty, some Chinese princesses were being sent to central Asia as brides for tribal leaders, to help keep the peace. One wrote about living in tents and drinking fermented mare's milk, and about her unhappiness: "My family has married me in this far corner of the world ... My thoughts are all of home and my heart aches within." A bit later, some Chinese Buddhists began traveling extensively. One monk, Xuanzang, ranged widely in central Asia and India, during the seventh century, ultimately bringing back to China a wider knowledge of Buddhism and information that also could encourage merchants to expand their orbit for exports and imports. Xuanzang's published *Report on the Western Region* was a major source of information for Chinese political and economic leaders, while popular versions of his travels (fancifully including a heroic monkey and greedy pig in his travel party) entered Chinese folklore.

The new religion of Islam actively encouraged travel and encounters with strangers, from the seventh century onward. The great annual pilgrimage to Mecca, urged on all believers if possible at least once a lifetime, brought people together from all over the vast Islamic world. For a few, the pilgrimage could inspire further wanderings. Several travelers also wrote accounts of their journeys, which expanded knowledge of key parts of the world and could promote imitation. Probably the greatest traveler of all time, Ibn Battuta, a lawyer from Morocco, got his first taste of adventure during an initial pilgrimage in 1325. Battuta came to love going to new places, often at the expense of amazingly long and difficult journeys (crossing steep mountains on the way to Mongol-dominated Russia in winter was just one of his exploits). He often got jobs during his journeys, thanks to opportunities in Islamic law and bureaucracy, and once in a while he married someone only to divorce her when he was ready to move on. All in all, during his lifetime, he would travel over 76,000 miles by foot, donkey and boat, going through the Middle East and the Byzantine Empire, plus much of central Asia, India, Sri Lanka and the Maldive Islands, West Africa, Somalia, and parts of China and Southeast Asia. He seemed to enjoy almost all his stops, except China where he never felt comfortable:

> China was beautiful, but it did not please me. On the contrary, I was very worried by the fact that the heathen have the upper hand there. When I left my house, I saw countless dreadful things. That disturbed me so much that I stayed home and went out only when I was forced to do so. When I saw Muslims in China, I felt as though I was seeing my own kith and kin.

Encounters, obviously, both in the past and today, do not always generate uniform delight. Even so, Battuta claimed he traveled fairly widely in China and commented excitedly about the great ships the Chinese were able to build. And Battuta's travel account, enthusiastic on the whole, was one of a growing number of documents that could inspire other people to catch the travel bug.

Contact drama is not just a pre-modern phenomenon. After American and British fleets forced entry into Tokyo harbor, beginning in 1853, far-sighted Japanese leaders began to realize they needed to learn more about this intrusive force from the West. Even before Japan officially adopted a reform policy in 1868, a few people – some of whom would later take a lead in redefining areas like education – began visiting the United States and Europe. The encounter was both challenging and important: challenging, because the Japanese had developed no extensive international experience at all for over 250 years, important because these were intentional study trips designed to guide new national policies for the future. Japanese visitors were impressed with Western technology, though they quickly and correctly realized that they could learn to replicate much of this. They were also dismayed at how much Westerners, and particularly Americans, threw away and wasted. They were deeply interested in Western science and openness to new learning – these would become themes in educational change. But they didn't care for what they saw as undue freedom for women (at a time when, many historians have argued, Western women were rather confined to domestic functions): they thought women were being given a level of respect that actually should go to older people, and they were not persuaded that this made sense. They were also deeply puzzled by parliamentary politics, or how people could argue so fiercely in the halls of congress but be friendly with each other. Overall, these pioneer observers began to identify Western traits that Japan probably needed to copy, but also a host of features that could and should be ignored or shunned.

LARGER THEMES

Part of the exploration of contact in world history does involve seizing on some individual stories – trying to figure out what people in earlier times might have learned from travelers' accounts, or measuring the impact of encounters like the exploratory Japanese visits. The larger approaches to encounters – which are what we review in this section – are ultimately more important, and there are also some standard basic patterns (the following section). Both the approaches and the patterns provide a useful orientation to the contact cases themselves.

GOOD AND BAD

Historians don't commonly use value-judgment terms like good and bad, partly because they shy away from this kind of moral verdict and more because most historical situations are complicated, with mixtures of benefits and drawbacks. It would not be sensible to spend too much time on good-bad evaluations concerning encounters. But it's pretty clear that some contact situations really harm some of the participants. Native Americans, encountering Europeans and Africans and their diseases, died off at an appalling rate over a two-century span. Add to this the shock of being pressed into unfamiliar political and religious systems, which manifestly left some Native Americans out of the new mainstream, and it's hard to find a lot to cheer about. There were new foods, weapons, domesticated animals, and some Native Americans adapted these fruits of contact quite creatively, but the trade-off was not good. (Interpreting the same encounters from a European standpoint would yield a different evaluation. Some contacts have clear winners and losers.)

Obviously, "bad" contact outcomes were particularly likely when encounters involved huge inequalities, though even here it's important not to exaggerate powerlessness. Disease and loss of property were the most blatant vulnerabilities in encounters with better-armed intruders. But (and the American experience demonstrates this as well) contacts might also involve an outside ruling group trying to press new standards of behavior that would alter private lives in disadvantageous ways. Many Europeans in the early modern period, shocked at the apparent independence of Native American women, urged husbands to discipline their wives more vigorously – to create more European-like domestic arrangements, which led in turn to a reduction in options and opportunities for expression for many Native American women.

"Good" encounters provide the groups involved with the chance to learn new techniques or expand cultural horizons, even amid a certain amount of tension in defense of older ways. On balance, the Japanese interaction with the West after 1853 was arguably a good thing. It certainly helped Japan preserve independence, by adopting new policies and technologies quickly enough to prevent outright Western land-grabs (as was happening in neighboring China). Once

Japanese enthusiasm for massive imitation was modified, for example by new policies in the 1880s, in the interests of preserving certain distinct Japanese values such as group loyalty, a fruitful balance was struck between reform and continuity. Of course there were some Japanese who thought even so that too much tradition was being sacrificed: there were intellectuals making this argument even in the later twentieth century. On the whole, however, most historians and, almost certainly, most ordinary Japanese at least after the first shocks of change would agree that modern encounters have benefited Japan.

LEVELS OF IMPACT

Not all encounters are equally meaningful. Travel accounts, for example, are fascinating examples of interaction, at least for the individuals involved, but they did not necessarily generate significant change. Ibn Battuta's life reveals the range of geographical connections that were becoming possible by the fourteenth century, but it is not clear that his excursions had extensive results. It's not even certain, in fact, how much Battuta himself was changed by his experiences, given his tendency to view other societies through a fairly strict set of personal values. Ibn Battuta's writings did gain readership, but most educated Muslims already knew a good bit about the regions he described. In contrast a European traveler to China, just a century before – Marco Polo – wrote an account emphasizing Chinese achievements that reached a Western European audience that knew far less about the rest of the world; here, the information he provided about his encounters really could stimulate new thinking and motivate additional efforts to reach out. It was no accident that Christopher Columbus carried a copy of Polo's book on his first voyage, seeking a new route from Europe to Asia. Individual encounters and their aftermath, in other words, generated results whose significance varied according to context.

It's sometimes not easy, even when larger groups are involved, to figure out what kinds of adjustments a new set of contacts produces. An intriguing contemporary example involves global tourism. Opportunities for people to visit distant places increased greatly in the contemporary period of world history, particularly with the advent of jet travel from the late 1940s onward. Significant numbers of Westerners and, soon, Japanese and others began visiting natural wonders or historic sites around the world. Many regions, from Thailand to the Bahamas, geared their economies extensively around global tourism. But was the result a significant encounter? In 1950 a Belgian entrepreneur founded Club Med, designed to develop resorts in southern Europe and, soon, in other sun-drenched spots like Turkey or Malaysia. The settings were distant and exotic. But Club Med was at pains to organize Western-style accommodation for largely Western guests, serving largely Western cuisine. Once a week, local cooking was trotted out for variety, and excursions could be organized off the compound to visit non-Western sights. But Club Med placed a premium on limiting the amount of adjustment its guests would have to experience. Hopefully, the result was usually a good vacation. But was it a significant contact experience for the Europeans involved?

The same question, more surprisingly, applies to local populations who serve the global tourists. It might be expected that maids and waiters who attend wealthy foreign tourists would have their lives turned upside down, with new material expectations and exposure to strange habits. Most studies suggest, however, that at least for a while local workers are not deeply affected. They go home to their villages and families and largely turn off what they saw during their stint at work. Over time, however, with a younger generation, dress styles often change (and become less modest), as youngsters interpret contact differently and use it to free themselves from some parental controls; and sexual habits can also shift.

Still, the overall point is clear: not all contacts matter as much as might be imagined. They may be cushioned by people sticking together, in their own familiar ethnic and family enclaves, and ignoring a new setting around them, and they may be modified by the sheer force of traditional disapproval.

Two tasks, then, in assessing contact experiences: try to decide what the balance is, between undesirable and desirable consequences (admitting that this may involve some value judgments that go beyond an objective historical record); and second, try to figure out if the contact had significant effects or whether, for various reasons, it largely bounced off those who were most involved.

DURATION AND INTENSITY

A third aspect of any contact experience figures into the evaluation of impact: contacts may be of various durations and intensities, and short ones, usually, are less important than those that are more prolonged. The European crusaders operated in and around Jerusalem for a few decades. They were influenced by exposure to a more advanced urban setting, as we will see below, but it's actually not clear that local Islamic populations were particularly affected save insofar as the Europeans directly attacked them. Muslims certainly formed some additional impressions of the European intruders – sometimes admiring their bravery, sometimes deploring their violence and their lack of the true faith, sometimes finding them clumsy and unsophisticated. But they did not take much away from the contact that affected life once the Europeans were gone. Local habits were too deeply ingrained, and the whole experience was too brief to matter much. In contrast, when Chinese merchants and scholars began to develop new interactions with India late in the classical period, it led to several centuries of exchange and student pilgrimages around the incorporation of Buddhism into Chinese religious and artistic life. Even though the Chinese government ultimately turned against Buddhism, and reduced its visibility, significant consequences persisted because the exposure had simply been too extensive to be easily erased. Important Buddhist minorities combined with wider recollections of Buddhist teachings and the influence on styles in art and architecture.

RANGE

Encounters can have all sorts of results. They can help a population learn about new techniques or foodstuffs. They certainly influence styles. Russian nobles, during the period of Mongol control, widely adopted Mongol costumes and particularly hairstyles, including a characteristic pigtail. When Peter the Great, fresh from extensive personal visits in Western Europe, sought to redo the nobility toward more Western norms, he insisted on a conversion to Western styles, presumably cutting off some pigtails himself. Contacts affect trade patterns. Initiatives from North Africa early in the post-classical period, including some outright raids, helped show

West African merchants the potential profits in directing more trade toward and across the Sahara – which amplified contacts still further. Encounters can alter scholarship, bringing students across borders to take advantage of unfamiliar learning. Thus East Asians headed to Buddhist centers in India to learn; European scholars in the post-classical period flocked to Spain and Byzantium to gain access to classical and Arab materials; West African interaction with Islam led to the creation of a scholarly center in Timbuktu; students from various parts of the world acquire access to Western institutions today.

It is tempting to argue that contacts are particularly interesting, particularly deep, when they also go on to affect basic cultural patterns, social forms, or political institutions – areas that in principle might be seen as particularly resistant to change and outside influence. Thus Japan's careful imitation of China in technology and high culture, during the post-classical period, did not result in a full adoption of Chinese practices toward women, though Chinese ideas had some influence. China today is abundantly open to foreign models in business or technology, but wants to keep external political patterns at bay. Yet there are cases where encounters are so extensive and durable that they affect private life or politics as well as other areas. Where contact spreads religious conversion, for example, it is clearly going to spill over into family patterns. Russia's experiences of Mongol control, though it led to fierce dislike of the overlords, probably affected the styles and expectations of subsequent Russian rulers – though the extent of this political legacy has been debated. As with duration, taking careful stock of how many areas of human activity were, or were not, affected by contact offers some fairly precise measurement tools for figuring out what the encounter was all about.

ATTITUDES AND RECEPTIVITIES

Different societies, in different time periods are more or less open to learning from encounters. Some ruling groups embrace diverse interactions as a source of interest and potential advantage. Mongol leaders were widely tolerant of various outsiders, and so were the early Mughal rulers in India. Japanese policy, from the post-classical period to the present, has alternated between interest in outside models and retreat. Western society in the post-classical period, though hostile to Islam as a false religion, was fairly open in its interest in imitating various aspects of Islamic society as it was encountered through trade or other contacts: interactions thus affected Western patterns from philosophy through architecture and commercial law. But by the fifteenth century Western Europe began to be less willing to acknowledge Islamic influences (though it still learned from contacts in some areas, such as coffee drinking and the public functions of coffee houses). More broadly, by the early modern period Western observers began to downplay the achievements of most other societies with which they were in contact, particularly because of the apparent inferiorities other societies exhibited in technology.

In some cases, attitudes can actually spur policies that prevent contacts in the first place, as when Japan so decisively limited both foreign access and international travel around 1600. At least as interesting are cases in which dominant social values discourage certain groups from learning much even when contacts occur, because of assumptions of special superiority. Here again are opportunities for explicit assessment as part of the larger process of determining what a given set of contacts involves.

CHANGE OVER TIME

Probably the most challenging general theme to keep track of, in dealing with contacts as a basic feature of world history, involves change over time. There's no question that the pace of contacts has quickened in every successive world history period. This is, after all, a basic feature of the larger periodization scheme itself. More societies encounter each other, and over longer distances, and more frequently, in each succeeding era. This means in turn that technologies that support contact change, and, though harder to measure, motivations shift, with more awareness of the advantages to be found in deliberate contact efforts. The easy part of this theme, then, involves simply tallying up how encounter patterns in one period differ from those of another.

The more basic question, however, involves the issue of disruptive change. Were there some points, in world history, when the pattern of contacts shifted so decisively that the nature of the human experience altered as a result – not just in one society, but more widely? Some world historians, emphasizing how interactions have been a constant part of world history, really want to stress continuity: while admittedly the incidence of contacts shifts, the basic phenomenon sails steadily forward. But we have also seen different approaches. Historians who emphasize developments around the year 1000 as a divide, with differentiation predominating before that point, convergence based on expansion and more deliberate acceptance of contacts predominating thereafter, are pointing to decisive changes in the contact experience. Experts who highlight the fundamentally innovative qualities of recent globalization have yet another take: they too are arguing that contacts begin to revolutionize culture and institutions, but for them the dividing line is recent.

These are difficult issues, precisely because contacts can be traced so early in human history – they are clearly not just a modern invention – and because aspects of their incidence and impact are hard to chart precisely. Scholars, obviously, disagree. But the underlying question is valuable even so: as contacts are assessed over time, are there points at which a boundary line can be drawn to denote change in nature, or do the stories flow on in a more gradually cumulative fashion? Here is a way to pull together some of the more specific themes about impact, duration and range.

MUTUALITY: ENCOUNTERS AS RECIPROCAL

A final set of standards concerning the world history of contacts involves not just assessment themes, but some basic findings that have emerged from the growing body of scholarship on interactions – including scholarship explicit to world history.

For one of the big contributions of the expanding interest in what happens when one society in some fashion encounters another – learned partly from anthropological work on other cultures, as well as from world history itself – involves the recognition that whenever serious contact occurs, there are impacts from and on all the parties involved. Contacts are mutual experiences and they produce mutual compromises and adjustments.

This is particularly important to insist upon when contacts involve significant power disparities. Thus the famous episodes of

European imperialism, in the late nineteenth century, used to be interpreted in terms of European impositions on so-called native peoples, since without question Europeans held dominant military, political and diplomatic power. The only issue might be the extent to which certain populations managed to escape full European control. In fact, even imperialism was an interactive process, in which local populations managed to express themselves in many ways, rather than simply responding to European directives, and the Europeans involved were affected as well.

There are several facets to this general expectation that contacts, even among unequals, will generate complex interactions and not mere imposition from above.

First, even very powerful groups rarely want to risk trying to impose too much, when they are in contact with a presumably "subject" population. They might generate too much resistance in the process, and/or jeopardize the profits they derive from the contact. British authorities in Nigeria, for example, tried to be very careful to conciliate the largely Muslim populations in the north, during their period of imperial control. They frequently sought to restrict Christian missionaries and other reformist elements, even those coming from Britain, basically on grounds that local Islamic authorities kept good order and did not attempt to mount systematic resistance to loosen British controls and that therefore they should not be bothered. Both French and British authorities were very hesitant to interfere with practices in some African regions, like female circumcision, that they disapproved of but where there was risk of popular protest if reforms were undertaken.

Further, and fairly obviously, any significant contact situation does not generate uniform encounters. Rural populations, widely scattered, are often less affected than urban groups (this remains true even today, for example with exposure to external consumer influences). Some groups will work, often effectively, to curry favor with a powerful external source, others will hold back. A powerful modern Nigerian novel, *Things Fall Apart*, shows how some groups (in the southern regions) were immediately attracted to aspects of Christianity in the late nineteenth century. Mothers of twins, for example, who risked seeing their children put to death as symbols of evil in local polytheistic beliefs, might seek shelter in the outside religion. Young people might find opportunities for expression precisely because their fathers did not yet participate. But adult men, with the most powerful positions in the pre-contact order, were most likely to be hostile, most likely to try to stay out of the contact orbit.

The first point, then, in exploring contact or encounter situations where power imbalances are involved is to recognize that even apparently conquered groups are not usually put under maximum possible pressure to conform. Further, experiences with the contact, and motives for reaction, will vary considerably among different groups.

The second point involves looking at how even apparently dominant groups are also shaped by contact, even when they may claim that their values are superior and should be left untouched. Food choices provide an interesting example from the experience of Europeans in the Americas by the sixteenth and seventeenth centuries. As Europeans reached the Americas, they discovered a host of unfamiliar foods. Their encounter with the potato and corn, and other delicacies like chili peppers, would have a huge influence on global eating patterns as – through contacts with Europeans – societies like China and Africa gained access to some of the foods. Europeans themselves, however, were food conservatives for quite a while, and shunned most of the New World offerings (they still largely disdain corn, as "animal food"). But Europeans in the Americas – the people most directly involved in contact from the Old World side – made a number of adjustments, besides just bringing Old World foods across the Atlantic, which they also did. Although there were complaints about the dryness of some Native American uses of corn, European-Americans quickly found ways to make it more desirable. (Native Americans, for their part, criticized European bread, which also seemed too dry, "like eating a corn stalk" as one of them noted.) Fairly quickly, important food fusions occurred. Americans began to use pork fat to lubricate traditional corn dishes like tamales, and Europeans began to enjoy these too. Use of chili peppers and American beans quickly defined a new, Latin American approach to cuisine, which often combined with food products of European origin. Here, then, is a case where European standards long proved rather immune to the results of a new encounter, but where Europeans-in-contact, though clearly part of a ruling class that could have held out for greater food purism, adapted rather quickly, joining native, lower-class elements in creating mixed menus that in turn would long define – indeed, that continue in some ways to define – differences between American and European food uses. The general point is this: in contact situations, look for mutual impacts, and not just impositions from one group to another. Whatever the power position, it's hard, in extensive contact situations, not to be affected to some extent – hard not to change habits at least to a degree.

The third point also addresses power disparities in contact situations. When the contact is extensive, in terms of duration and an involvement of significant numbers of people, even the most powerless groups will normally find a way to preserve some independent self-expression and through this will have a larger impact on the encounter itself. Sometimes, in a contact, some people are so clearly abused, so obviously unfairly treated, that it is tempting to imagine that repression is the only result. And perhaps there are cases where this is so. Certainly there is often a problem of evidence. We have little record of the experience of slaves seized from Europe and sent to the Middle East in the post-classical period: there was contact, but we don't know its dimensions. When Indo-European migrants and invaders entered India, conquering and repressing local populations (often, probably, with considerable violence), we simply have no direct evidence about what opportunities remained for the locals, save that many of them turned up at the lower ends of the caste system. Where we do have evidence, however, the proposition normally stands: even in situations of great inequality, contact is almost always to some extent a two-way street. This is why, in world history, the experience of conquered groups, for example Africans under imperialism, must be studied in terms of interactions and not just impositions.

A classic, and significant, illustration of the general proposition comes from the experience of slaves of African origin in the Americas. We know that slaves were seized with great brutality and subjected to massive hardship and disorientation in the slave ships, and then frequently forced into demeaning and demanding work and, often, further disruption of whatever family ties they attempted to form. Sexual exploitation was often considerable, and slave owners frequently attempted to limit access to such tools as literacy. Yet, in all this, the standard parameters of a contact situation still applied. African slaves helped create a new food culture in the Americas by bringing over crops such as watermelon, black-eyed pea, eggplant and okra, which soon made their way into plantation kitchens as well as the slaves' own food supply. Use of ham to flavor soups was another African contribution that soon became part of American cooking. Rhythms of popular music owed much to African roots, and ultimately these would translate into ragtime, jazz and even rock. African fashions influenced quilting patterns and clothing designs, again for populations well beyond African Americans themselves. Contemporary rap music shows the survival of African oral traditions of storytelling.

In parts of Latin America like Brazil, where slave populations were even larger than those in the United States Deep South and where European Americans were less racially prejudiced and less bent on cultural regulation, African impacts were even more substantial. Brazilian music would owe much to African dance and rhythmic traditions, including drumming patterns. A Brazilian martial art, *capoeira*, was rooted in African patterns. African religions also had great force, combining with both Native American and European traditions to create new religious syntheses. Several Brazilian religions that emerged in the nineteenth century, like *Candomblé* and *Umbanda*, blended various beliefs. Africans had brought their gods with them, and summoned them with various customary dances and chants. Even though the rituals were attacked as pagan, they not only survived but attracted audiences beyond the Afro-Brazilians themselves. Then, when the Brazilian Republic legalized these religions as part of a new separation of church and state, in 1889, the combinations came into their own, both in secret rituals and in public ceremonies. Hundreds of thousands of people today profess these African-shaped religions directly, and many more combine their practice with more orthodox Christianity. The point is clear: not only did oppressed groups survive contact by preserving some of their own folkways, which is important in itself; they also actively contributed to contact by providing material culture, art forms and beliefs that would attract many other people in ways that helped shape the whole society.

The final standard outcome of encounters – and the most important one, in summing up results of the first three features and more besides – involves introducing the word *syncretism*. Most encounters of any significance produce blends from the various groups involved that preserve some previous traditions (again, from all the groups involved at least to some degree) but that represent a new amalgam, a change to some degree for all parties. This is how contacts alter human history, not usually by overwhelming all the standards of one group by those of another or sweeping all prior patterns away, but by forming new mixtures. Syncretism − "the combination of different forms of belief or practice" − most efficiently describes this common result. So, whether the word is used or not, whenever an encounter or exchange is being explored in world history, look for the syncretic outcome. Obviously, there is no way to predict exactly what the mixture will be: in this sense every encounter has its own story. But predicting that a syncretic mixture will be there is a very safe bet.

Examples abound, from early encounters to ones that were occurring yesterday. Cooking, in American civilizations, mixed local, European and often African elements: it was a syncretic brew. When, under Alexander the Great, Greek scholars and officials operated for over a century in Bactria (northwestern India, part of present-day Pakistan) they influenced local art so strongly that for many decades artistic representations of the Buddha featured Greek-style robes and hairstyles. Religion was not dislodged by Greek beliefs, but a new syncretism defined the way it was presented. When Jesuit missionaries reached China and India in the sixteenth century, seeking in principle to spread Christianity, they quickly adopted local costumes and habits to such an extent that it became difficult to know whether they were converting or were themselves converted: syncretism, here, applied to individual lifestyles in a contact setting.

Syncretism may take unexpected forms. The period of the Christian crusades, from the late eleventh century onward, overtly expressed hostility to Islam and to Islamic control of Jerusalem. The crusades led to considerable violence against Muslims and various reprisals in return. The whole episode would not seem a particularly good candidate for a syncretic result. And indeed, there is little record of the crusading Christians adopting much from Islam itself or vice versa. But the crusaders did learn about the urban material standards that were commonplace in the Middle East, but a far cry from conditions in the more primitive cities of Europe at the time.

So they increasingly combined Christianity with a new level of interest in material comforts and accompanying trade levels, which affected not only their own tastes but economic and social patterns back home. An unexpected syncretic result, but a genuine and important one nonetheless.

China's long interactions with Buddhism generated fascinating examples of syncretism. Many Chinese sincerely and deeply converted to the new faith. But to make way in China, Buddhist leaders also made some significant adjustments, emphasizing more clearly women's inferiority and family obligations and also the importance of loyalty to the state. The result was a different type of Buddhism from that spreading in other areas – a clearly syncretic version that mixed change and continuity, from the Chinese perspective, in intriguing ways.

Syncretism is alive and well in the contemporary world, amid all the external pressures associated with globalization. Japan takes an American television form, the game show, and adapts it to the special national traditions of group conformity and shame: when a contestant goes astray, as a result, he or she may be subjected to group disapproval, or shaming, that Americans would normally find unacceptable and contrary to personal dignity. McDonalds, one of the great United States contributions to current world food cultures, obviously spreads change: the chain, and others like it, encourages faster eating, cleaner surroundings, and more superficially cheerful service than many regional traditions had emphasized. But change must be mixed with adaptation, so that a syncretic McDonalds results. Restaurants in India feature more vegetarian fare than McDonalds back home. Those in Japan have introduced the teriyaki burger. McDonalds in Morocco puts on special meals, after sundown, during the Islamic fasting month of Ramadan, emphasizing traditional fare more than burgers during this period. McDonalds in France must serve beer at least, if not a bit more.

Exploring syncretism, as contacts multiply in recent history, offers a targeted means of analyzing the local and the global, one of the basic habits of mind world history depends on and seeks to inculcate. It certainly offers an obvious focus for inquiry that jump starts a coherent approach to the whole encounter phenomenon. Here is the final, and most significant, rule of thumb to guide analysis in this vital world history area.

CONCLUSION

The long record of encounters and their results forms a central core in world history. It encourages analysis of change over time – both in tracing the results of specific contacts and in evaluating shifts in basic contact patterns. It organizes comparison, in terms of determining how different societies or civilizations responded to contact opportunities plus assessing how different groups reacted to a particular contact experience. While contacts require individual evaluations, there are some shared standards of measurements that can make their study more coherent. And there are some usual results, in very broad terms, that above all encourage the engagement with contacts in terms of mutual interactions and syncretic outcomes. Some of the most interesting as well as significant features of human history are wrapped up in the gives and takes of interactions across the boundaries of any single society.

FURTHER READING

Many good resources are available on cross-cultural interactions, including Jerry H. Bentley: *Old World Encounters: Cross-Cultural Contacts and Exchanges in Pre-Modern Times* (New York: Oxford University Press, 1993); Greg Dening, *Beach Crossings: Voyaging across times, cultures and self* (Philadelphia: University of Pennsylvania Press, 2004); Xinru Liu and Lynda Shaffer, *Connections Across Eurasia: Transportation, communication and cultural exchange on the Silk Roads* (New York: McGraw-Hill, 2007); Masao Miyoshi, *As We Saw Them: The first Japanese Embassy to the United States* (Berkeley: University of California Press, 1979); Stuart B. Schwartz, *Implicit Understandings: Observing, reporting and reflecting on the encounters between European and other peoples in the early modern era* (Cambridge, UK: Cambridge University Press, 1994); and David Northrup, *Africa's Discovery of Europe 1450–1850* (New York: Oxford University Press, 2002).

7

TOPICS IN WORLD HISTORY

World historians spend a good bit of time defining time periods in their field, and also regions and major societies. As we have seen, they do not always agree, but they do recognize the importance of discussion and transparency. The picture is less well developed when it comes to the topics, or types of human activities, that world history emphasizes. This chapter explores the kinds of topics that world history almost always covers, but also how it is expanding its topical range and, finally, how the field might potentially embrace even more subjects in future.

A tension here is obvious. Just as world history in principle covers all places at all times — but in fact tries to select more coherent and manageable emphases — so world history in principle covers any significant type of human activity, wherever it enters the historical record. Furthermore, history as a discipline has been rapidly expanding its list of researchable topics over the past half century, particularly through the growth of the field of social history. We now have serious historical work on childhood, crime, old age, death, leisure, food habits, even sleep. Can world history include a list of this sort? At what point does the expansion of topics become unmanageable?

World historians generally agree that a few types of topics simply must be dealt with. Trade patterns form an obvious case in point. Major political structures have to be included. Big cultural systems, like the leading religions, are unavoidable. Topics like environmental history are also gaining some traction. But there is less agreement on how to handle certain other types of historical topics, including some of the newcomers on the social history list.

THE STAPLES

CONTACT TOPICS

Several common topics, recurrent in most if not all world history periods, promote the exploration of contacts among major societies. *Trade patterns* – no surprise here – constitute the most consistent contact theme in world history, from signs of interregional exchange before the classical period – for example, between India and the Middle East – to the intense commerce that today forms the backbone of globalization. Knowing the role and evolution of interregional trade is a world history essential. With this comes attention to the technologies involved in trade (shipping and navigational devices) and relevant commercial organizations as well, like the great trading companies of the early modern period or the multinationals of the later twentieth–early twenty-first centuries.

Other contact topics are also important, but somewhat more sporadic. The development of *missionary religions*, cresting in the centuries after 600 CE, is a vital cultural facet of the larger focus on encounters. Additional developments in the early modern period, especially in the interactions of Christianity with populations in the Americas, and then signs of the spread of science and new political ideas in the eighteenth–nineteenth centuries keep the *cultural contact* topic going.

Attention to contacts also involves key elements of *diplomatic* and *military history*. Before modern times there were only a few military campaigns that significantly cut across regions, but they certainly deserve attention: Alexander the Great's efforts and the massive Mongol conquests are obvious cases in point. Greek–Persian and later Roman–Persian battles; Arab military expansion; Arab–Chinese warfare in western China in the eighth century; Chinese territorial expansion and tribute relationships with neighboring states; the short-lived European crusades in the Middle East; Turkish and Russian expansions would form a representative list of cases where military efforts pushed beyond a single region or civilization.

Western conquests and imperialism from 1500 to 1914 headline the modern interregional military agenda (including the Seven Years War, 1756–63, as a first "global" conflict), but recurrent Russian–Turkish warfare and the American wars of independence merit attention. Headed by the two world wars, the interregional military list expands noticeably in the contemporary period. Regular diplomatic interactions are primarily a modern topic, as the practice of sending representatives and negotiating among distant states began to become common from the early modern centuries onward. There are however a few antecedents, as in tribute visits to China. By the nineteenth century, finally, the topic of international diplomacy must also encompass the beginnings of outright international organizations, like the International Postal Union or the Red Cross, and obviously this innovation expands much further in the twentieth and twenty-first centuries.

Migration is a growing interest, though here too major developments are sporadic rather than consistent over time. Initial travels of *Homo sapiens sapiens* out of Africa; Indo-European migrations in the 2nd millennium BCE; Slavic, Bantu and Turkish migrations as highlights stretching into the post-classical period constitute an initial list. European migrations plus the forced migrations of the Atlantic slave trade pick up the topic in the early modern centuries. Fueled by new transportation systems and global population growth, the migration theme, especially from poorer regions toward industrial areas, forms a major theme from the nineteenth century to the present.

Interregional disease transmission is the final common contact topic, of major importance but happily recurrent rather than constant. The role of plagues in the later classical period, the bubonic epidemic of the fifteenth century, and the spread of disease to the Americas in the sixteenth to seventeenth centuries are obvious milestones in this thematic area. Epidemics in the nineteenth century, such as cholera, deserve attention as well, along with new public health, medical and global-organizational responses, and this mixed theme carries into the contemporary period of world history.

Societal structures. The second set of stable topics may involve contact patterns, but the topics relate more to basic characteristics of major societies themselves. These topics – beginning with political structures – allow key changes and continuities within major societies to be traced (like a shift from feudalism to more centralized monarchies in Europe between the post-classical and early modern periods). They also support comparisons, with attention to shared or parallel developments as well as differences among civilizations. Sometimes, finally, the same topics do also capture the results of contact, as when one society tries to copy the political structure of another or when, in modern times, larger movements seek to export particular political systems (whether Marxist or democratic) across regional borders.

A good way to approach this second set of common topics involves asking what functions any complex society must perform. Thus every society needs to organize power relationships, and in civilizations this occurs at least in part through a formal government structure. Figuring out the nature and functions of government – *political history* – is an obvious topical standard. Every society generates an effort to explain physical nature and the purpose of human life, which in turn involves core beliefs and assumptions and also artistic representations – in short, every society has a *culture*. Every society organizes production and trade – the *economic* aspect of the society's history. And every society defines social relationships and inequalities, making *social history* a final essential in any topical list.

POLITICAL HISTORY

Political structure typically leads off discussions of state organization in world history, after the rise of formal government of any sort.

Periods of empire, and societies that tended to favor empire, form a clear theme. Empire is both a form of government and an expression of expansion, and both aspects are important. Until the advent of European overseas empires, the imperial form usually involved considerable centralization, at least by pre-modern standards, and relatively large bureaucracies. The office of the emperor itself was surrounded with considerable authority and ritual, and sometimes claims of divinity.

Less centralized political forms include city states and princedoms (as in classical Greece and often in India), though these sometimes embraced an intense local political life. Loosely-organized monarchies – as in Russia or sub-Saharan Africa in the post-classical period – were also common. The special political characteristics of feudalism (during part of the Zhou dynasty in China but also post-classical Western Europe and Japan) form another option.

The past several centuries have witnessed a wider set of political options, along with the gradual decline of monarchy and empire. Waves of revolution (late eighteenth to early nineteenth centuries and the twentieth century) mark key changes. Democracies and new forms of authoritarianism are important developments in the past two centuries, along with the rise of more modern forms of parliaments and the idea of constitutional protections for human rights. The surge of nationalism from the late eighteenth century onward, and its global spread, is an important innovation in its own right, but it can relate to several different forms of government organization. Tracing the emergence of the nation state is a related modern theme with global resonance.

Along with government structure, however, several other political topics deserve consideration, though they are less often highlighted in world history. The *functions of government* are at least as important as government form, though the two features are usually related. Some governments claim extensive functions, beyond the usual commitment to defend territory and to offer a system of justice and crime control (and, of course, to define some sources of tax revenue). Many early governments tried to enforce particular religious or cultural systems, and the relation between religion and the state, and degrees of tolerance, form a crucial topic for many societies.

Some states have clearly been more warlike than others, and key changes both in military organization and the nature of war form a vital facet of political history. Different government structures help generate shifts in the size of armies. Technological change is a vital element in altering war and the military – most obviously with the advent and evolution of guns, but earlier as well. Modern military change also links to other alterations in government functions, for example in taxation and economic controls or in propaganda.

Government forms and functions can be focused through an effort to characterize what the relationship was between a state and ordinary people – what voice people had (if any), where they could expect government to intrude on their lives, and what they expected states to do. State-people relations vary among societies and change over time. One of the key shifts in modern political history is an increasing government impact on a wider range of activities.

CULTURAL HISTORY

The culture category has fewer subtopics than the political, but there are some special complexities as well.

For most agricultural civilizations, the major religion or religions form the most obvious starting point for getting at beliefs and assumptions, which are in turn the main focus of cultural analysis. The religions expressed ideas about nature, human nature and society, as well as spiritual and ethical concerns. Some understanding of polytheism is also essential to grasp cultural contexts prior to the rise of religions like Buddhism or Islam, and also to identify lingering remnants even after conversion to larger faiths. Confucianism – a philosophy rather than a religion – obviously played a leading role in organizing cultures in East Asia, and in the classical Mediterranean philosophy requires consideration alongside religion.

For more recent times, religions, while still important, have found competitors for the provision of broad cultural frameworks. Ideologies like Marxism or nationalism but also the cultural assumptions surrounding consumerism require attention here.

Most societies generated *political theories*, sometimes in relation to religious ideas, about the role of the state but sometimes separately as with Confucianism. This topic bridges between culture and politics per se. Changes in political theory in modern times often involve interregional contacts and influences.

Along with dominant cultural frameworks and political beliefs, the role of *science* forms a vital element in cultural analysis, including its role in organizing knowledge about physical nature and disease, the relation between science and religion, and the implications of science for technology. The massive redefinition of science and its role since the seventeenth century, ultimately on a global basis, is a major factor in overall cultural change in modern world history.

Leading *artistic styles* – at least in painting, sculpture and architecture – form the final main cultural topic for world history. Different societies had different signature styles in these areas, and there has been change over time and important instances of interregional influence.

Cultural history, finally, explores relations between "high" culture – the work of leading thinkers, religious leaders, or artists – and popular culture – the beliefs and styles of ordinary people. Usually the two cultural spheres relate to each other, but also, usually, imperfectly. Ordinary people often have different ideas about nature (including magic) or beauty from what their leaders urge on them. High culture is easier to identify and describe than popular culture is, but some attention to the relationship is essential in understanding what a culture is really about, and the tensions and overlaps are intriguing in their own right.

ECONOMIC HISTORY

Besides trading patterns, economic topics include *technology* and *technological change*. Different societies develop different levels of technology for agriculture, manufacturing and transportation. Technological change includes patterns of mutual influence and imitation. Military technology may be seen as a partially separate theme, but it often has economic impacts as well.

Roles of *merchants* and cities vary. All complex societies develop some urban centers and trade specialists, but their size and their status vary from case to case and of course they change over time.

Agriculture and *manufacturing* form obvious subtopics. Agricultural patterns involve specific crops and animals, technology, labor systems, and levels of production (surplus). Manufacturing history focuses most obviously on the industrial revolution and its steady global expansion – still in process. Preindustrial societies had craft (artisanal) and rural manufacturing systems that deserve attention.

Labor systems vary considerably in both agriculture and manufacturing. Slavery (in several forms; this is not a single institution over time); serfdom; and wage labor are the most common options, often in combination. They can be compared, and changes from one system to another are often key aspects of economic change more generally. Labor systems include, finally, differential but variable roles for discrete segments of the population: women, children and the elderly.

Economies can be variously organized. *Economic systems* also help shape labor structures and technologies and vice versa. Manorialism, focusing on relations between landlords and serfs, can be a key economic system; so can estate agriculture. Capitalism is clearly the most important economic system in modern world history, though it takes various forms in different times and places. The rise of capitalism, initially in commerce but ultimately in agriculture and manufacturing, is a key change in world history and deserves explicit analysis. The rise of socialist movements and some socialist economies in the nineteenth and twentieth centuries allows exploration of alternative efforts in economic organization. The development of global economic institutions, particularly since World War II, forms part of contemporary economic history and the history of capitalism broadly construed.

SOCIAL HISTORY

All complex societies introduce various forms of social inequality, between groups and between the two genders. These forms reflect but also help shape political and economic systems, and they have a profound cultural dimension in ideas and assumptions about how it's proper to organize and justify inequality.

Class structure is a key starting point. Various societies offer different systems, from castes to classes, with different economic and political positions for each major group. The existence or absence of significant slavery is another obvious variable. Definitions of the *upper class* or classes vary, and this is another entry point into social structure. Opportunities for *social mobility* diverge as well.

Race, along with class, factors into systems of inequality. Historians debate how much race mattered, or was even identified, before modern times. There are no firm conclusions about the role of race in Roman or Arab slavery or the Indian caste system, though the discussions are compelling. With the rise of Western imperialism, and especially in the nineteenth to twentieth centuries, claims about race took on greater importance in defining social structures, within societies and globally alike.

Growing interest in *women's history* has deeply affected scholarship in world history over the past 20 years, though gaps in analysis remain. The rise of patriarchal systems, combined with various specific implementations of this system in the major societies around the world, set up some subtle comparative issues during the long agricultural phase of world history. In every society, differences between upper and lower classes factor in, in terms of actual women's roles, cultural opportunities, and birth rates.

As always, change requires attention in the women's history/ world history connection. What general impacts, if any, did the spread of the missionary religions, with their claims about spiritual equality, have on gender relations? How much have industrialization and the spread of new ideas about women altered the types of patriarchy characteristic of agricultural societies?

Attention to women leads to some discussion of *family systems* and potentially to ideas about masculinity as well. These topics, however, are incompletely developed in world history coverage so far, compared to analytical through women's roles and status. There is some coverage of major family types – for example, nuclear (parents and their children) as opposed to extended (grandparents, aunts, cousins); and there are periodic references to *kinship systems* (vital in African social history). These categories lead to some additional comparisons among societies and also further assessment of patterns of change – like the impact of industrialization and the rise of cities on traditional extended family relationships.

Table 7.1 Topical Checklist – for major societies and for change and continuity over time

Contacts	Politics	Culture	Economics	Social topics
Trade	Forms of government	Religion	Technology	Class structure
Culture	Functions – including military	Political theory	Role of merchants – cities	Race (where relevant)
Diplomacy/ War	Major protest	Other value systems	Labor systems	Gender structure
Migrations		Science	Agriculture/ manufacturing	Family structure
Disease		Artistic styles	Environment	Demography
Global institutions (for 1850s ff)				

The one vital aspect of family history, broadly construed, that world history does highlight consistently is *demography*, or population patterns. Big variations in birth and death rates, and resulting age structures, contribute to comparisons among major societies and also between upper and lower classes. The interaction between demography and migration is another key connection. Above all, tracing the impact of the rise of agriculture and then its more recent displacement by more industrial economies on basic demographic patterns – the rates of birth and death – provides some crucial markers in world history.

SUMMARY

While it's vital to have a list of major topics in mind, world historians also track their interrelationships – how in modern societies, for example, religious beliefs affect demographic behavior; how ideas about women or changes in technology help shape political structures. It's the combination, along with analysis of cause and effect relationships, which adds up to larger definitions and which feeds comparisons of the major societies, and it's the same combined analysis that ultimately helps in accounting for world-historical change and periodization.

OTHER TOPIC AREAS

Any appreciation of world history must acknowledge the need for innovation in topics, as the field keeps pace with broader developments in the discipline and changing needs in the societies around us.

Food history is gaining interest as a revealing aspect of individual societies and, certainly, as a way to trace the human impact of contacts. The subject is not yet an essential in world history, save in particular instances like the Columbian exchange, but it may expand.

The key new entrant is environmental history, as global environmental impacts, environmental debates, and efforts to develop new methods of control become a vital part of our own world. One of the key attractions of Big History is its placement of the human past in the larger unfolding of the earth's evolution. Even apart from Big History, most world history programs now include some attention to environmental impacts in the past, even in some hunting societies and certainly with agriculture. Environmental considerations become part of the examination of individual societies and cultures – there have been quite diverse ideas about human responsibilities toward nature in the past as well as today – and as part of the definition of key world history periods. Environmental history gains importance from the industrial revolution onward (including the effects of industrial demand for raw materials on areas like Africa or Brazil). The exploration in recent history inevitably pushes up against the bitter contemporary political debates over topics like global warming. The topic is still taking full shape, as research findings expand, but it's definitely becoming part of any core list.

WORLD HISTORY AND TOPIC EXPANSION

Wider topical expansion is NOT part of the standard world history agenda, at least to date. It's important, for example, to know something about consumerism as part of the past 150 years of the human experience, but not (yet at least) essential to identify a pre-modern consumerist history (though it's very interesting). There is not enough time to cover everything, and we don't yet know enough about some topics, on a global basis, to push them forward.

Still, there is and should be a tension between any list of world history topics and what that list might ultimately become, with additional topics and changing priorities. A valid part of the world history experience should include some notion of how to embrace additional topics, without insisting that the standard list be indefinitely expanded.

Childhood offers a case in point. Except for attention to demography, childhood is rarely referenced in current world histories (most textbooks either don't have the subject in the index, or offer a single reference or two, usually when dealing with educational systems as part of modern political and cultural change). But historians of childhood are reaching out for fuller geographical coverage, and a further mutual link with world history may develop.

A world history of childhood already generates a plausible overall framework. The context for childhood and the functions of children change considerably with the advent of agriculture, with growing work obligations and larger family size, and then they change again with industrialization and the increasing emphasis on schooling. Here are two familiar but essential landmarks that help set up this new topic. Comparison is also important: different societies defined the specifics of childhood differently; there were even variations in common practices such as (in early agricultural societies) the use of infanticide. The spread of world religions created some general changes in childhood, such as new encouragement for religious training and an attack on infanticide. More recently, other cultural-political innovations, like communism or consumerism, also leave a mark on childhood. At least in recent history, contacts, including ideas about some common global obligations to children, also play a role, connecting childhood to this aspect of world history.

A massive set of new topical additions to the world history list is NOT looming right around the corner. Rather, we can expect ongoing innovation and rebalancing. And it is clear that world history can contribute to additional topics and be enriched by them. Knowing at least how to get a start on an unfamiliar connection expands the analytical capacity of the field.

CONCLUSION

Gaining a sense of what topics to apply to particular civilizations or time periods is the final step in developing a world history roadmap – along with identifying key regions and time periods themselves. The topic list does not predict what to find – boxes like government functions or environmental impacts must be filled in for each case – but it does provide guidance in what to look for. The same list, as we have seen, can shape comparisons – where similarities as well as differences must be embraced. It also helps chart change and continuity over time: does a new period include changes in gender relations, and if so how does this link to other key developments? Local/global analysis gains focus when applied to specific topics as well. And finally the topic list has its own dynamic side: along with some staples, identification of topics can and will expand, and this process helps adjust world history both to changing concerns in our own societies and to new discoveries about the past.

FURTHER READING

On migrations, see Patrick Manning, *Migration in World History* (London: Routledge, 2005); on trade, Kenneth Pomeranz and Steven Topik, *The World that Trade Created: Society, culture and the world economy, 1400 to the present* (Armonk, NY: M.E. Sharpe, 1999); on the environment, Stephen Mosley's *The Environment in World History* (London: Routledge, 2009). On culture, see Donald and Jean Johnson, *Universal Religions in World History: Buddhism, Christianity and Islam* (New York: McGraw-Hill, 2007); on science, James E. McClellan, III and Harold Dorn, *Science and Technology in World History: An introduction*, 2nd ed. (Baltimore: Johns Hopkins University Press, 2006).

8

DISPUTES IN WORLD HISTORY

We have seen, in Chapter 3, that one of the habits of mind that historians work on involves the capacity to handle historical debates or differences in interpretation. Controversies over social issues are commonplace in our own day. Figuring out how to manage different views about past topics – from identifying what kinds of evidence are used, and how adequately, to assessing the logic of arguments, to exploring opportunities for analytical synthesis or compromise – can contribute to a vital intellectual skill that is important well beyond the history classroom.

This chapter does not try to list all major or possible world history debates, for there is no agreed-upon list of Controversies That Students Must Know. Debates about periods and, even more, regions (and civilizational choices) have been covered in previous chapters.

DEBATES IN THE DISCIPLINE: WHY ARGUE SO OFTEN?

Scholars, historians prominent among them, like controversies. Debating past research and analysis helps knowledge move forward, though admittedly some arguments can get personal and many can become rigid or silly. Still, challenging received wisdom, on the basis of new evidence or new patterns of analysis, does on balance improve understanding. Even when the challenges are a bit excessive, and some compromise or amalgam is ultimately possible, they can shed additional light and force a useful testing of established arguments and assumptions.

In history, many debates focus on causation: why did a major change occur? A classic debate, that has some bearing on world history, concerns the origins of World War I. Right after the war, all sorts of observers jumped in to say that the war was really Germany's fault, for being too aggressive and too dependent on a fixed military plan, but others said that France and Britain must share some of the blame for not clarifying their positions earlier and more forcefully. This particular debate obviously had diplomatic as well as scholarly implications, and it ultimately became rather pointless. Improvements occurred when historians – mostly, a new generation not wrapped up in the horrors of the war itself – began turning away from trying to assign national fault and looked to more basic factors like the excesses of European imperialism or the dependence of industrial capitalism at that point on heavy military expenditures and distractions from social issues. By this point, a century after the war, arguments have largely ended and a deeper context for understanding the emergence of the conflict is widely accepted.

World history, as a field, has not actually generated as many intense debates as have more conventional areas like Western diplomatic history. The newness of the field, as a major focus within the history discipline, helps explain this: surely more classic debates will emerge as world history expands and matures.

WORLD HISTORY AND THE WEST/UNITED STATES

One endemic debate involves approaches to the West, for world historians collectively continue to struggle over the issues involved. From the world history standpoint, the felt need to reduce the amount of attention collectively assigned to the West can take on a certain amount of belligerence. And some world historians are so eager for correctives to the conventional, West-centered account and so hostile to anything that smacks of Western superiority that they belabor Western faults disproportionately – a process called West-bashing. The *National Standards* for world history issued in 1994 thus clearly, and arguably legitimately, highlighted Western failings such as the Atlantic slave trade or racism, but carefully exempted any of the other civilization traditions covered from any critical assessment: only the West, a simple reading might suggest, has ever introduced global harm. The new interest in environmental history may sometimes similarly fall into this trap of disproportionate West-bashing, as if Western experience and values alone bear responsibility for environmental degradation.

Some of the debates about world history obviously operate at an overall curricular level: should world history courses be required instead of the old Western civilization diet? How can we get beyond patchwork projects that still overdo Western coverage, in favor of more genuine world history focus? But some discussions, about how to introduce critical assessment into the treatment of nonWestern societies at a time of obvious international sensitivity and understandable resistance to Western self-righteousness, install important controversies into the world history project itself. How, for example, should the involvement of African merchants and governments in supplying slaves for the Atlantic trade in the early modern centuries be handled? In addition to the obvious need to correct false stereotypes about Islam and women, are there nevertheless some aspects of the historical record that raise more complicated issues?

An important set of arguments, then, revolves around the problems of rebalancing the conventional focus on the West and related assumptions about the special merits of Western values, along with the delicate exploration of complexities in other traditions. As with the old arguments about World War I, debates in these areas are both scholarly and political, with important contemporary implications, which make them particularly challenging but also unavoidable.

The *place of American history* in a world history project extends this debate area still further. Significant efforts are underway to revise conventional treatment of the national experience in terms of internationalization. From the world history standpoint, a crucial potential debate emerges over how much the United States, as it gained greater global power from the late nineteenth century onward, behaved in a distinctive fashion or basically followed patterns set by older powers like Britain. Here is a way to move the controversies over American exceptionalism into more global terms.

CLASSIC DEBATES

A massive number of controversies have been raised in earlier historical scholarship that obviously have world history implications, even though the debates did not begin in a world history setting. This is where the list might become dauntingly long, depending on the amount of time and attention available. A few examples can suffice to indicate the nature and utility of a larger category. In several cases, world historians can not only tune into established discussions, but can amplify them through connections with the wider field.

THE ROLE OF INDIVIDUALS IN HISTORY

This used to be a big topic, and it remains valid. The history of any region, and certainly world history, offers many examples of extraordinary people, mostly the powerful but once in a while dramatic ordinary individuals as well. What role have they played in history? Do individuals usually cause much by their own actions, or are they mainly factors amid larger forces? A few world historians have studied individuals, like the traveler Ibn Battuta, and have used biography to speculate about individual impacts. Conquerors, like Alexander the Great or Chinggis Khan, most obviously come to mind in thinking about individuals who changed the course of things (in 1999 a sober magazine named Chinggis Khan the most important person in all of world history over the last thousand years), so that's a way to focus debate. But other individuals, in other areas of achievement, can spark discussion – for example, when thinking about the reasons for the industrial revolution, do any individuals matter very much? Or was it all a matter of larger forces?

THE ROLE OF ORDINARY PEOPLE

Partly because social history is newer than the other standard topical areas, and partly because social history sometimes moves according to different time patterns from political or cultural developments, some world historians have been tempted to downplay it. And here's the resultant debate: how much is it worth exploring the ways in which lower classes and women are oppressed, so long as one knows that they are poor and oppressed? India had a caste system, Rome had slavery, but does the distinction matter very much either to the way the people involved lived, or how their societies functioned? Do differences among different slave systems – slavery in the Arab world, for example, compared to Atlantic slavery in the early modern period – matter particularly, since by definition they all involved a common lack of legal freedom? The debates here, in other words, focus on the roles of ordinary people and the significance of the specific details of the systems that ensnared them. The same issues easily apply to women: if you know that all agricultural societies are patriarchal, do differences in the precise nature and tone of patriarchy matter very much? Even in more modern times, are ordinary people best viewed as victims or as positive actors who help shape the environment around them?

AFRICAN HERITAGE

We know that classical Greece sent travelers to Egypt and elsewhere, among other things to study mathematics. But two decades ago a scholar claimed more than this, arguing that Greek science, art and culture were largely derived from Egypt and Mesopotamia. Greek historians were quick to refute, claiming that Greek achievements were largely owing to local genius. The controversy is intriguing: it involves best judgments about the available facts but it can also be affected by a sincere desire to give Africa more positive attention, or conversely to make sure European creativity still gets special credit. The debate is worthwhile, in forcing evaluation of the difficult question of pre-classical heritage but also possible contemporary prejudices, but it does not yield an easy call.

THE FALL OF ROME

This is an old discussion that began actually when observers saw the western part of the Roman Empire crumbling around them. Historians picked up the challenge variously over the past several centuries. Explanations have included sunspots (now discredited), the role of Christianity in undermining Roman virtues (now discredited), or some law of history that dictates that every civilization must ultimately collapse and die (now at least complicated). Debate currently centers over the priority to assign to outside invasion and internal issues (including what we now know were really serious epidemic diseases). Along with this, the role of anti-social changes in upper-class habits, deterioration of leadership, and corruption of the populace still compete for attention: it's hard to ignore shifts in human behavior as part of the equation. Finally, a number of historians have been seeking to put the Roman case into a larger, recurrent category in which territorial overexpansion undermines domestic strength and sends a society tumbling. This inquiry does not suggest some sweeping historical law, but a number of specific cases that can put the Roman factors into a broader causal context and thus expand the historical debate.

ISLAMIC POLITICS

Various scholars have tried to generalize about the political principles that followed from Islam, given the fact that the actual governments of the Arab caliphate never corresponded fully to stated ideals. Contemporary issues have intruded, leading to some claims that Islamic principles are incompatible with democracy – and counter-arguments that point to considerable flexibility and also to the fact that no religion was initially geared toward democracy. Here is a tough controversy, inherently complex and now sensitive as well, that obviously contributes to a world history project, and not just a regional one.

THE ROLE OF THE CRUSADES

European historians once debated about whether the crusades signaled a significant development and expression of new strength, or a distraction and minor interlude. This debate has now expanded, thanks in part to world historians' interest in the patterns of trade and consumerism that seem, unintended, to have resulted from new European contacts. Some debate over impacts within the Islamic world – partly fueled by new, purely contemporary sensitivities to the word crusade – can supplement older fare.

MONGOL IMPACTS ON RUSSIA

Russian tradition emphasizes the strangeness and barbarity of the Mongols, and how Russia finally and triumphantly threw off their yoke. But Russia had been changing even before the Mongols arrived, so not all problems need to be tallied to the invaders. And then there's the difficult question of how much the Mongol experience shaped Russia for the future, for example in the political arena or in military aspirations.

CHINESE EXPEDITIONS

Why did the Chinese end their Indian Ocean expeditions at the end of the 1430s? Here's a good causation discussion with implications for Chinese trading roles more broadly. Some historians point to fairly specific factors: a new emperor who wanted to chart his own course, competing concerns about building a new capital city and enhancing the Great Wall. Others – not entirely disagreeing, but taking a larger view – claim that Chinese distrust of the outside world, and a Confucian/bureaucratic tendency to disparage innovation and particularly commercial innovation, were at play. Decisions here are important, as to whether this important decision reveals some fundamental flaws about traditional China or merely some shorter-term considerations.

"AMERICAN" DECLINES

Figuring out why Mayan civilization stumbled, well in advance of European pressure, or why Aztec and particularly Incan empires encountered troubles right before Spanish arrival raises a host of interesting causation issues, complicated by the lack of fully adequate evidence (though there's more to go on than in the case of Harappa earlier). Discussions range from reactions to political oppression to problems with water sources and other environmental factors.

EUROPEAN EXPANSION

European historians have usually framed the European voyages of discovery in the fifteenth century in terms of a new, dynamic spirit associated with more ambitious governments and the spirit of the Renaissance. Specific questions about why Spain and Portugal led the way may be attributed to the role of individual leaders (we have seen that world history raises interesting general issues about points at which individuals really shape their times) and the results of Christian re-conquest of the Iberian Peninsula. Putting this debate into world history terms, however, raises additional issues concerning the results of European borrowing of Arab and Chinese technologies (sail, compass, guns) and also particular European problems in finding funds to pay for desired Asian imports. Several scholars have recently argued quite vigorously that the European achievement was far less a matter of any distinctive Western spark than simply how much the Europeans had copied (sometimes without much acknowledgment) from Asia. The result is an old-new debate important in world as well as European history.

INDUSTRIAL REVOLUTION

Figuring out what caused the industrial revolution, and why first in Britain, is another old debate that can now be recast. Classic ingredients included the rise of imaginative (disproportionately British) inventors, the expansion of banking, plus new laissez-faire economic doctrines and a new entrepreneurial spirit. These components now receive less emphasis, though they certainly fit some political interpretations about what best promotes economic growth. Instead, more impersonal factors like population growth and changes in state policy now enter in. Historians who discovered an eighteenth century but pre-industrial expansion of consumerism in Europe added a vital new component, based on solid evidence: new levels of demand helped cause the industrial revolution rather than the other way around. World historians, here too, can use this debate, which is partly about individual genius versus broader trends, but they can also add to it, particularly in pointing out the role of prior expansion of foreign markets and the capital earned in world trade. Recent work also highlights how Europeans decided they had to innovate technologically to match, for example, Indian costs in producing cotton cloth. Expanded debate can thus now include rebalancing purely European versus global factors from the very start.

EMANCIPATIONS

From the 1940s onward, historians have been debating why slavery began to end. One West Indian scholar urged that the answer was economics pure and simple: slavery was inefficient in the kind of capitalist and early industrial economy that was surging in the first decades of the nineteenth century. This approach has not been entirely discarded, but there is substantial empirical evidence against it. More recent scholars have highlighted and tried to explain the rise of a new humanitarian spirit, and attention to slave unrest has also been factored in. Cynics have added the possibility that early factory owners deliberately used slavery to distract their own societies from labor abuses closer to home. This is a great debate about choosing among, but also balancing, quite different kinds of factors. Increasing awareness of the limitations of emancipation, including racism and continued exploitation, and also the role of growing global populations in supplying alternative labor add desirable complexity and also a more global, rather than purely Atlantic, scope.

IMPERIALISM

Debates over what caused imperialism have raged since the late nineteenth century. Some scholars (including Marxists and even Lenin himself) have pointed to industrial economics: the need for assured markets, investment opportunities and raw materials amid advancing capitalism. But various scholars have sought to debunk this, among other things through empirical arguments about how much the colonies cost and how most international investment actually focused not on colonies at all, but on places like the United States, or how most industrial exports went to other industrial countries. But the economic explanations refuse to die. Alongside them, or possibly in their place, other scholars have posited the importance of national rivalry and diplomacy within Europe; the role of individuals, including both aristocrats now uncomfortable in their industrial homelands and sheer profiteers. The role of the mass press and even claims about boredom and the need for vicarious adventure in industrial societies enter into the mix. Recently, gender history has contributed discussions about changes and challenges in Western masculinity, but also the roles of women in helping to shape the imperial enterprise.

This old debate, still capable of innovative contributions, obviously fits into world history quite nicely. Again, world history can also contribute. Along with the European factors, world historians pay more attention to the kinds of allies imperialists could acquire in expansion zones like India or Africa – imperialism becomes something more than a purely Western venture, requiring probes into the complexities of the receiving societies as well.

World history simply cannot pick up all the intriguing controversies, for lack of time. But selecting some of the more revealing discussions and often pulling them into a broader and more interactive context form a vital part of world history analysis, and a suitable introduction into the demanding art of making sense of disagreement.

THREE BIG DEBATES

Three major disputes about basic interpretations go beyond issues associated with world history periods, regions and topics in raising questions worth grappling with. Two of the disputes are well-established but certainly not entirely resolved; the third is newer, just taking shape, with dimensions that cannot yet be fully determined.

WORLD ECONOMY

A variety of scholars, from several disciplines, have collaborated to generate what's been called world economy theory, but the approach has been most closely associated with sociologist Immanuel Wallerstein.

Here's the gist of the theory: Wallerstein and other world economy analysts argued that as world trade levels began to rise after 1500, with the inclusion of the Americas, durable inequalities also began to emerge in the commercial relationships among key regions. On the one hand, a series of *core* societies took shape – initially Spain and Portugal, later northwestern Europe. *Core* societies exported finished products (like guns); they dominated the trading companies that carried world trade, and they also built the ships. There was money to be made in all three of these outlets. Core societies also had unusually strong governments and military forces – they used this strength to muscle into other parts of the world, and trade profits helped fund larger governments in turn. They also developed wage labor economies, which facilitated worker mobility and flexibility. Core societies, obviously, gained disproportionate wealth from world trade, although internal allocations maintained large pockets of poverty among the workers.

Peripheral societies – initially, Latin America and the Caribbean – were the mirror images of the core. They exported cheap foods and raw materials, and had to import most manufactured goods, losing money in the transaction. They had small merchant classes (because the core handled trade) and scant shipbuilding. Obviously, though peripheral societies might generate individual wealth for mine owners or estate owners, the societies as a whole suffered in world trade, even though they could not escape its tentacles. Governments were weak, because core societies did not want local interference and because estate owners also worked to prevent any controls over their operations; and also because tax revenues were scant. The periphery, finally, depended on low-cost, coercive labor systems, like slavery or the kind of serfdom imposed on natives and mestizos in the mines and estates of Latin America (and also the southern colonies in the British holdings in North America).

World economy theory also includes an intermediate type of society, *semi-peripheral*, and finally designates some societies – like Russia at least until the eighteenth century – as *external*, strong enough to stay out of deep international commercial relationships and therefore not defined by these relationships. By definition, other than relative noninvolvement, not much can be predicted about the characteristics of the external cases.

This is a powerful theory, and it has won many advocates. It has several potential advantages. First, it explains relationships among different aspects of a core or peripheral society: if one knows what the export-import situation is, one can also predict the basic level of government and also the nature of the labor system. Second, by the same token the theory facilitates comparison. If two societies are core, regardless of superficial differences, they will have huge similarities in economic, political and labor features, and the same holds true for components of the periphery. And the theory automatically frames any comparison between a core case and a peripheral case. Third: the theory can capture expansion of the basic categories. By the eighteenth century, for instance, Poland, with a weak government exporting cheap grain to Western Europe, had many of the same peripheral features as Latin America did, despite huge differences in geography and prior history. And examples of this sort can easily be multiplied – for example, by seeing Japan as a nation that became part of the core by the mid-twentieth century. Finally, and this was what motivated Wallerstein in the first place, the theory helps explain continuity over time. Once a society achieves core status, it will likely stay that way, because wealth and strong government tend to perpetuate themselves. To be sure, Spain and Portugal did not hold their position, falling toward the semi-periphery; but Britain, France and other societies that moved into the core have persisted very well. Even more important, lack of revenue, merchants, skilled labor and effective government makes it very difficult for a society to leave the periphery, and arguably there are parts of Latin America even today that locked into the periphery in the early modern period and still are fundamentally described by this position.

But the theory has encountered many objections – this is where the debate comes in. For many, perhaps most world historians, the objections have overshadowed the advantages of the theory. But the controversy is still interesting and relevant, important in itself and illustrating the kind of sweeping arguments about the shape of world history that helps train in debate management and can illuminate key issues – whatever side one ultimately takes.

The theory oversimplifies: Britain and France were both core by the seventeenth century, but France had a far larger and more centralized government. The political differences may well have overridden shared core characteristics. West Africa, enmeshed in the slave trade, may have developed a peripheral economy like that of Latin America (seeing slaves, unfortunately, as cheap exports), but West African governments were far stronger than their American counterparts through the early modern period.

The theory omits cultural characteristics. Many economic historians do in fact believe that societies respond to basic economic factors with no cultural input: a recent book thus discounts any role for science or modern culture in explaining why Britain was first to industrialize, looking strictly at labor and energy costs and rational economic response to these. But many world historians would argue that relationships between, say, Western Europe and the Americas or Africa were shaped by beliefs and values and not just cold calculations.

The theory does not clearly explain change. It's easy to see, once a society has changed, where to put it in the world economy categories, but not always easy to determine why and how it changed in the first place (as in figuring out why Spain fell out of the core).

None of these objections is fatal, but they add up to important questions about precision, and many world historians prefer a more sensitive exploration on a case by case basis.

But the big attack on world economy theory, at least for the early modern period, involves the question of characterizing most of Asia. World economy theorists believe that Western Europe obtained an unjust advantage in world trade — it's easy to use the theory as part of West-bashing — but they also emphasize how powerful this region became. Many world historians argue that attributing this much clout to the West, at least before the long nineteenth century, is simply inaccurate, another example of failing to escape the trap of Western-centric historical analysis. And they do not protest simply as a matter of principle. They further claim that world economy theory fails to acknowledge the great success that China and India had in world trade well into the eighteenth century and beyond. China, after all, gained more silver from world trade than any Europe power did, and India was in second place. China was not exactly core: it did not control the commercial companies or shipping that carried exports and imports. But that's precisely the point: it does not fit world economy theory, and its exceptionalism — plus its great importance in the early modern economy — means that the theory is not simply in error, but actually does more harm than good.

So: can the theory be fixed or modified to take care of some of the problems, or is the whole effort so cumbersome that historians should jettison it (as many have)? Can debate about the theory actually be made useful in exploring world history, not just in the early modern period but also (as Wallerstein argued) in dealing with global economic inequalities in the nineteenth century and beyond? Different historians will react differently to these issues — that is, after all, what debate is all about. Exploring the controversy and possible resolutions remains a very useful exercise — beginning with understanding why each "side" in the discussion takes the position it does.

MODERNIZATION

This theory is older than the world economy approach, and at odds with it in several respects. The theory took shape in the 1950s, among various American economists and social scientists, though it built on earlier work such as that of the great German sociologist Max Weber.

While there are several specific versions of modernization theory, the idea focuses on the changes that have to go along with, or prepare, the industrial growth of an economy and attendant economic change. Governments must become more efficient, with more specialized training and merit selection for the bureaucracy – this is a key aspect of political modernization that accompanies or prepares economic change. Modernized governments need to pay more attention to public health and education. Military modernization obviously includes up-to-date weaponry and training techniques, and more merit-based selection for officer promotions. Families must modernize, at least to the extent of reducing the birth rate, for excess population will retard modern economic growth. The new levels of education are essential – here is a political as well as a social facet of modernization, along with greater emphasis on scientific subjects. Many modernization theorists would also contend that gender gaps must close, at least in terms of access to training and meaningful work. One of the questions about modernization theory involves its extent: how many institutions and behaviors does it cover?

There are several potential advantages to modernization theory, which is why it has been widely used despite some fuzziness around the edges. First, it connects different patterns of change, arguing that they're part of a general package. Thus the theory can be applied to Western history over the past three centuries, to show how educational change, for example, related to industrial development which in turn links to reforms in civil service (bureaucratic) recruitment. Similarly, the theory can help explain why, when Japan launched its huge reform effort in 1868, it focused on military change, public health, education, gender relations (to a degree) as well as economic change per se.

Second, many modernization theorists argue that the theory has a predictive quality: it anticipates that more and more societies will jump on the modernization bandwagon and in the process introduce changes that follow along lines already established in the West, Japan, and elsewhere.

Finally, some modernization theorists, extending the prediction element, have also used modernization to ask questions about why some societies are slow to modernization – to identify what special problems might be involved. Thus Turkey, which began to try to modernize under Kemal Ataturk in the 1920s, made heavy going of the process compared to Japan. What, some theorists wonder, was wrong: was it the religious context or some other set of issues? An interesting book explores Chinese history at the end of the 1800s in terms of barriers to modernization. Modernization, in sum, can be used to ask comparative questions, about why some societies move faster, or slower, than others.

On the other hand, many historians have objected long and loud to the modernization package, on several grounds. First, some argue that it doesn't even fit the Western experience itself. Economic growth, thus, was not evenly distributed: modernization theory can make it seem that everyone involved gained male middle-class type benefits, whereas in fact the experience of workers or of women must be differentiated. The easy equation between education and industrialization, others argue, is simply factually wrong: many uneducated workers participated strongly in industrialization, and the claimed correlation is at best inexact. These critics dispute, then, the first advantage of modernization theory, in positing connections among different types of activity and historical change.

Even more venom is directed at claims about modernization processes outside the West. There are two additional points here: first – and world historians can easily predict this one – the whole theory makes it look like the world will become, or should become, as much like the modern West as possible. Critics argue this is wrong both as a goal and as a historical measurement: lots of societies don't want to become the West, can't become the West, and/or shouldn't become the West – take your pick. World economy theorists might specifically argue that the theory underplays how extraordinarily difficult it is for peripheral societies really to modernize, and it's their peripheralization, not their incipient modernization efforts, that should receive primary attention. And finally, many critics shudder at the idea of research projects directed at failures to modernize, as if certain societies are somehow stupid or retrograde, or at the possibility that these condemnations might become part of serious historical evaluation.

Modernization theorists have unquestionably become more beleaguered in recent decades. Among other things, modernization ideas, applied by American invaders first to Vietnam, then to Iraq, have not worked out smoothly: it turns out that importing modernization and expecting a quick and enthusiastic result simply does not work. But there are still some centers of modernization theory, and the term and idea continue to be used informally despite all of the caveats. Russian history surveys, for example, routinely refer to Peter the Great as a modernizer (if he was, he was a highly selective one, not an across-the-board reformer, so there's need for caution about this pervasive reference).

Updated modernization theorists would argue that it is possible to distinguish modernization from down-the-line Westernization. Japan is a truly interesting case in point: it arguably modernized, but neither its culture nor its politics became fully Western. China may be another example right now: it modernizes vigorously in many ways but resolutely rejects the Western version of modern political structures. Distinguishing between modernization and Westernization is hard, and involves some active debates and subtleties, but it is a possibility.

Modernization theorists would also argue that, for all the problems with their approach, a global effort at modernization is precisely what has taken shape around us, with societies trying to reform educational systems, military structures, gender relations (at least to a point) and so on, with modern technologies and economic growth the key ultimate goals. There's a lot at stake in the tension between some suitably cautious modernization theory and the alternative plea to look as the histories of individual societies, over the past two centuries, on a largely case-by-case basis or through the lens of world economy categories.

GLOBALIZATION

This final category has potentially sweeping applicability to world history, just as world economy and modernization theories do. It's a newer debate area – the term globalization was introduced in English only in the 1990s, though the Japanese had a word 30 years before. It's not yet clear whether a big debate will ensue, as historians try to work the concept – developed by other social scientists – into a world history agenda. But there's strong potential, at least, for some interesting discussion.

Globalization is the process of "transforming local phenomena into global ones. … a process by which the people of the world are united into a single society and function together" – or, at least, it is a process that is rapidly heading in that direction. It involves integration of regional economies into a single international economy through trade, foreign investment, shared technology but above all shared participation in basic production and exchange processes. But it also involves unprecedented global cultural influences, for example in science and consumerism, and also unprecedented international political institutions and standards. It's a sweeping process, cutting across a variety of aspects of human societies.

The idea of globalization can be accepted without clear value judgment. Most globalization theorists, like most modernization theorists, have tended to welcome the developments they discuss, but it is perfectly possible to admit that globalization is occurring and deplore the results. As we have seen, international polls show in fact that most people in the world dislike globalization – 72% dislike its cultural aspect, 56% its economic aspect; only a bare 51% majority approves of political globalization (but most Americans would actively dissent from this one). Part of the debate over globalization involves identifying and balancing its advantages and disadvantages. This may be a process that continues to advance despite many downsides and despite popular dismay.

But the debate that's beginning to emerge in world history involves a different and indeed a classic set of issues: the timing and extent of change. The group of historians, calling themselves the "New Global historians", argue vigorously that globalization, over the past several decades (most accept the 1950s as the turning point), creates a dramatically novel historical context. The emerging "global epoch," in their view, ranks with the agricultural and industrial revolutions, or even higher, in terms of the extent of change involved. These historians point to a global economy as "something different: it is an economy with the capacity to work as a unit in real time on a planetary scale." They note that many multinational companies are larger and more powerful than most national governments, and they add the global importance of many international institutions and Non-Government Organizations in transcending conventional state and regional lines. Even popular anxieties shift, as people realize how much of their lives are determined now by faceless global forces. The new global historians conclude that only by realizing the massive extent of change can we develop ethics and humane standards to match the new world taking shape around us.

No world historian would deny substantial recent change; this must be built into any account of the current period in world history. But debate has surfaced about the extent of innovation claims, and two major alternatives have been put forward.

The first, and it's the most logical world history option, sees contemporary globalization as the latest in many stages of heightened contact among major societies around the world. Several recent studies take this approach. There's some defense of the transregional routes of the post-classical period as the real inception point, after which each subsequent intensification followed from existing motives − starting with the quest for greater profits in trade − and building on prior transportation technologies. If not 1000 as the beginning point, many would opt for 1500 − because contacts became global for literally the first time at this juncture, because commercial and military benefits became even more compelling and because governmental and business organizations clearly began gearing up for consistent contacts. One historian argues that the next bump should occur in the later eighteenth century, with still more-effective governments and capitalist enterprises, and with European manufacturing and consumerism both depending more regularly on global sales and supplies. Then, the additional transformations that define contemporary globalization would set in as simply the latest phase. Obviously, there can be considerable discussion of what stages matter most, but the real issue is whether the stages approach itself makes most sense as opposed to the idea of a truly dramatic departure during the past half-century or so. Arguing for phases does not depend on a sense that nothing is new: each phase did involve changes in technologies, organizations, motivations and impacts. But a pattern defined in terms of a series of phases is not compatible with the "new global" historians' effort to paint a truly unprecedented transformation.

Quietly, finally, a third approach has been ventured, though it can also be integrated into the phases argument. Several historians have urged that it's really the mid-nineteenth century, not the mid-twentieth, that sees the inception of globalization − not just an anticipatory stage, but the real thing. Changes in transportation, like the steamship, combined with tremendous increase in trade flows, the first signs of global political arrangements and institutions (like the system that facilitated international mail delivery), the spread of globally-popular sports, and even new travel-and-return types of migration to create the first effectively global framework. To be sure, as one main proponent puts it, this globalization was "nascent and incomplete", and it would be interrupted by a host of regional counter-reactions in the decades after World War I. But when globalization did more fully resume, by the late 1940s, it built on structures and experiences already fully available. It was a resumption, not a brand-new transformation.

CONCLUSION

World history does not yet feature a long list of fundamental issues and divisions. There are no well-defined, hostile camps. Interestingly – and perhaps, appropriately, for this field – no clear pattern of specific national approaches to world history has yet emerged. Efforts in Australia have emphasized work on historiography and uses of web-based teaching technologies, but they mesh well with efforts elsewhere. A European center of world historical training, at the University of Leipzig, touts a "European-based" approach to world history, and this might involve some sensibilities about Western achievements different from those in the United States. Several pioneer writers have been pushing world history in China. But national divisions surface mainly over the extent to which world history is acknowledged at all, in school programs, not what kind of world history should be preferred.

But while this is not a field torn by rival passions, there are important debates. The field can incorporate, and slightly redefine, discussions that first arose in more specific national or topical arenas. It generates discussions of its own, particularly around regional definitions. And it does promote discussion of some major efforts at generalization, from the world economy debate onward, that involve really interesting issues of evidence and analysis. Controversies here both sharpen larger skills in dealing with conflicting inter-pretations, and improve the grasp of major trends and patterns in the unfolding of world history itself. This, of course, is precisely what grappling with analytical tensions is supposed to accomplish.

FURTHER READING

Good works on world-system analysis include Andre Gunder Frank, *ReORIENT: Global economy in the Asian age* (Berkeley: University of California Press, 1998); Kenneth Pomeranz, *The World that Trade Created: Society, culture and the world economy, 1400 to the present,* 2nd ed. (Armonk, NY: M.E. Sharpe, 2005); Immanuel Wallerstein, *World-Systems Analysis: An introduction* (Duke University Press, 2005); and *The Modern World-System,* 3 vols. (Maryland Heights, MO: Academic Press, 1980). See also Craig Lockard, "Global History, Modernization and the World-Systems Approach: A Critique," in *History Teacher* 14 (1981): 489–515.

On globalization, Bruce Mazlish, *The New Global History* (London: Routledge, 2006); Robbie Robertson, *The Three Waves of Globalization: a history of a developing global consciousness* (London: Zed Books, 2003); and Peter N. Stearns, *Globalization in World History* (London: Routledge, 2010).

For other key debates, Martin Bernal, *Black Athena: The Afro-Asiatic roots of classical civilization,* 3 vols. (New Jersey: Rutgers University Press, 1987–2006); Seymour Drescher, *The Mighty Experiment: Free labor versus slavery in British emancipation* (New York: Oxford University Press, 2002); and Robert C. Allen, *The British Industrial Revolution in Global Perspective* (Cambridge, UK: Cambridge University Press, 2009).

9

WORLD HISTORY IN THE CONTEMPORARY ERA

Historians vary in their reactions to any invitation to deal with recent developments. Some historians are deeply interested in what went before and distrust too much attention to the present, that might dilute the devotion to the past and that inevitably includes involvements and partisanships that can color judgment. In world history, we have seen that a number of historians have been much more concerned with probing early origins than in linking directly to the world around us today. World historians as a group believe that their subject helps people understand the contemporary world, but they differ about how much they want to tackle current relationships directly. The more remote past may seem more fascinating, analytically safer, or simply a preferred alternative given the fact that all sorts of noisy disciplines focus on the present already.

This chapter, in looking at contemporary issues in world history and even (briefly) orientations toward forecasting is not, then, an absolutely standard component of world history basics. On the other hand, all complete world history projects delve into the contemporary era at least to some degree, and at the same time dealing with recent and current developments involves some special problems that deserve brief focus of their own.

Recent history offers some special challenges. In contrast to some of their instructors, world history students have been actively aware of at most a small slice of the period. Communication across generations can be tricky. Current world historians, for example, were often educated by people deeply affected by the world wars and even the depression. But the interwar years now seem a bit less decisive than they once did: the menace of Nazism, though not to be forgotten, is hardly as intense as it was some decades earlier. On the other hand, for students, the Cold War is not a remembered experience at all, so there's legitimate discussion about how much detail to provide to catch an audience up with what many instructors actively remember.

LESSONS LEARNED

A vital component of sorting out the contemporary period involves remembering analytical principles world history has emphasized well before one approaches any part of the twentieth or twenty-first centuries.

The most important first step in defining any period in history involves making sure the dominant themes of the previous era – in this case, conventionally, the long nineteenth century – begin to yield in prominence. And it involves making sure that new dominant themes can be identified. If a period begins with a dramatic event or set of events, that helps as well. A new period should generate possibilities for defining change – the new themes – but also for identifying continuities, both in individual societies and in the world as a whole.

The second key step in defining a period involves making sure that the key themes apply to a number of regions – though perhaps in different ways, and with different responses – and not just one or two. In dealing with recent developments it's vital not to assume that what one knows about patterns in one's own society translates automatically to the world at large.

The third key step consists of making sure that a number of key topics are applied to the period. Not every major aspect of the human experience changes with each period, but no period involves just politics, or just economics. There has to be some topical range, and a careful effort to see how many topics can be legitimately involved.

And of course there will be debate. Particularly in dealing with recent issues, one can expect a great deal of discussion and controversy about how to cut the contemporary cake. Debate should not prevent some decisions, but it should also encourage a willingness to test and defend any major propositions.

In approaching contemporary developments, in other words, it's really important to remember that we know a great deal about how to handle issues of timing and chronology.

BEGINNINGS

The first specific issue in dealing with contemporary history is a familiar one: when does the contemporary period begin?

The most common answer is very clear, and quite defendable: it begins with the massive disruption that was World War I. But at least two other options have been presented already. Some contemporary coverage pushes back to the second half of the nineteenth century. The importance of the maturation and spread of the industrial revolution, and the argument about the mid-nineteenth century beginnings of globalization, make this a plausible choice, even though no single event heralds the onset. The other option is to hold off until the middle of the twentieth century. This would allow focus on the most intense phase of decolonization movement and the obvious decline of European supremacy; on a related note, it would capture the economic advance of a number of societies, beginning with Japan and the Pacific Rim, and the relaxation (though not the disappearance) of previous world economy inequalities. And it would please those historians who argue for a dramatic recent onset of globalization.

It's important to remember that discussions of exactly when a period begins are not unusual, and the presence of several valid options can stimulate a healthy debate. The issue does not have to generate distracting confusion.

The common choice of World War I reflects the magnitude of the war itself, and the extent to which it launched new types of war and new levels of government assertion. The subsequent emergence of both Soviet and fascist governments owed much to the experience of government controls during the war itself. World War I also, as already noted, marks the beginning of the end for European imperialism and economic supremacy. It weakened European states themselves. It further encouraged nationalist protest outside Europe. It encouraged economic advances by the United States and Japan in part at Europe's expense. The war promoted change in various regions. Most obviously, the collapse of the Ottoman Empire introduced new splintering in the Middle East, with impacts clearly visible still today. The war also set the immediate context for the Russian Revolution, another shaping event in the twentieth century along with the two revolutions, in Mexico and in China, which had begun a few years earlier. Finally, though this is less directly associated with the war itself, the 1920s saw further advances in some of the technologies that would further build global connections: radio communication moved ahead, as did air transportation. Larger technological steps would occur after World War II, but it's fair to note a rather steady progression from this earlier point.

In sum: there's no reason to expect World War I to be dislodged as the real and symbolic beginning of a new era, though it was a grim start. The possibility of debating other options will embellish analysis, but there are valid reasons to see the wartime period as a break from the past, particularly in terms of world power relationships.

PAST THEMES RECEDE

Demonstrating that the contemporary era shifts gears compared to the long nineteenth century is not hard. The nineteenth century filled with Western industrialization and ensuing (but brief) global economic and military supremacy. The new era saw Western dominance recede. Military assertions were increasingly qualified by the rise of other strong military powers but also methods of warfare, like guerilla fighting, that could limit Western effectiveness. Western strength remained, but not with the ease of operations that had been possible under imperialism. Outright political controls from the West diminished even more obviously, as more nations claimed independence – a few between the world wars, and then a rush after World War II. And while Western economic activities remained vital, particularly with the post-World War II recovery of Europe, there is no question that the global economy became more complex with the advances of several other regions. Through industrialization, as with the Pacific Rim and more recently nations like China, Brazil and India; through control of valuable resources, as with the oil-rich nations of the Middle East; even through successful commercial agriculture, as with Chile, the gap between Western nations and much of the rest of the world began to narrow.

The inequalities of the world economy eased to an extent, as several regions figured out how to escape the worst kinds of dependency.

Just as the long nineteenth century had been defined in part by a distinctive power balance, so the gradual but incontestable undoing of this balance sets a new framework for contemporary world history. This crucial definitional test for a new period – showing the declining salience of prior themes – can be easily passed.

ANALYTICAL CHALLENGES

This said, four complications immediately emerge. The first is a standard issue, but one that deserves particular attention for the contemporary period: don't forget some ongoing continuities. The second, more peculiar to the twentieth to twenty-first centuries, highlights the obvious fact that, in contrast to every other period, we don't know the end result of some of the major themes of our own age. The third focuses on the particular uncertainties in charting cultural change and continuity. The fourth, finally, more prosaic but really important in terms of periodization, involves the unavoidable discussion of whether there are any overarching themes, as opposed to some discrete sub periods.

(1) CONTINUITIES

All new periods, particularly in their early phases, show connections to the past – even though some novel patterns begin to gain ground. With contemporary world history (or contemporary history of almost any type), it risks being too easy to overlook this aspect. The dominant emphasis in many contemporary cultures, including that of the United States, is on change. Most people believe that the pace of change becomes ever faster. This may be true – it's worth thinking about – but even so the emphasis on innovation should not overwhelm an appreciation of important continuities.

World history continuities that persist, even amid important new themes, come in two varieties. The first, involves elements of the power relationships of the nineteenth century. The West still musters disproportionate strength. It has taken particular advantage of opportunities to develop airpower, and though other societies now have significant air forces and missile programs some disparities remain. The West (including the United States) remains the society most likely to intervene militarily in other regions. Though formal imperialism is largely a thing of the past, Western political models and cultural influences are still quite strong. Western efforts to guide human rights programs or encourage democracies remain an important part of contemporary world history. While leadership in science and consumerism is now shared with other societies, there is still an important Western voice. At the same time, several societies continue to reflect power inferiorities inherited from the nineteenth century or before. Some parts of Latin America remain trapped in levels of poverty and economic disadvantage that recall the characteristics of the earlier world economy periphery, and the same holds true of many parts of sub-Saharan Africa where dependency actually increased in the twentieth century. Western exploitation in some of these regions is now joined by Japanese, Korean, or Chinese ventures, eager to take advantage of cheap labor and vital mineral and energy resources, but the basic pattern is a familiar holdover from the past. Not everything has changed in the area of world power balances.

The second continuity from the past – vital to build into any contemporary analysis – involves ongoing characteristics of many key societies or civilizations. Developments from many previous periods, in some cases going back to the classical centuries, contribute to shaping particular regions and the ways they respond to larger contemporary themes. Many people are still strongly guided by major religious traditions. These traditions have not been unchanging; many religions take advantage of contemporary communications technologies, and many also pick up new emphases. But elements of the Hindu, or Islamic, or Christian approach obviously spring from earlier roots. Earlier artistic styles, similarly, help define regional characteristics even today, along with important innovations. Previous political and social structures still leave a mark. India abolished its caste system in 1947, but continues to face issues of caste-related inequality. Racial tensions in a number of societies form a heritage from older attitudes and structures. Divisions over political systems touch base, in some cases, with older attitudes about the importance of order and authority – even though the specific political choices have changed with the decline of monarchy and empire.

Obviously, no society is shaped entirely by the past. The Middle East has substantially changed as a result of innovations as varied as oil revenues, the spread of educational opportunities for women, and the emergence of new nations. The region is the scene of important tensions and debates about cultural and political choices. Older values and institutions play a role, but within a dynamic framework, and this is true for all the major regions of the world. At the same time, different traditions do contribute to shaping the contemporary balance between the local and the global, and the continuities involved form a vital part of relevant historical analysis.

Consideration of the local and the global leads to a particular sensitivity to syncretic combinations in the contemporary world. At times, the embrace of change, and particularly the obvious interest that develops in many groups to take advantage of global influences, may seem to eclipse traditional elements. Often, however, even the new force of global contacts is colored by the need to blend prior values and institutions. As a result, creative syncretism is one of the most characteristic expressions of contemporary world history.

(2) OPEN-ENDED DEBATES

By definition, we lack perspective on the most recent period in world history, which inevitably invites discussion. We don't know the end of stories, as we do for all the earlier periods.

Take an obvious issue, recurrently debated: will the current period in world history turn out to be a story of the decline of the West – perhaps like the gradual and complex decline of Arab society beginning toward the end of the post-classical period? And if so, will another society (perhaps China?) rise to claim pre-eminence for a while? Or is the West's decline only relative – that is, Western society will remain vibrant but simply not as artificially dominant as it was in the nineteenth century? And if so, will the next period of history involve the interactions – tensions but also collaborations – among several major societies, rather than the pattern of singular dominance that obviously described the previous period? These are all good questions, well worth keeping in mind, but we simply can't answer them yet.

Or take a more subtle question, less often discussed but certainly ripe for debate. Will the current period in world history, thanks to the power of globalization, turn out to see a decline of separate civilizations in organizing institutions and cultures, with global connections finally predominating instead? Already, for example, many scientists, working across borders, identify with their intellectual training more than with their civilization of origin, and the same trends may be emerging in other areas thanks to ease of contact and new levels of travel and migration. Or will civilizations reassert themselves, narrowing identities and perhaps becoming less tolerant and more belligerent in the process? There are signs of this possibility as well, and indeed a vision of clashing civilizations (particularly but not exclusively the West and Islam) was the subject of a major discussion after the Cold War ended. Again, at least two sets of trends are both plausible and possible but we cannot yet know which will prevail. The story is not over, and in this case may not be very fully developed yet.

The last several decades have seen an unprecedented spread of democratic political forms, particularly in places like east-central Europe, Latin America, and parts of Africa. But several key societies have not been part of this trend, and others seem to hesitate. Will democracy continue to spread (thanks to global standards, the implications of new and more open information technologies, or other factors), or will global political diversity continue to prevail? Contemporary trends allow this kind of question to be posed – it would have been a bit of a reach to raise the question in 1900 – but they certainly do not generate an answer.

Will contemporary societies, collectively or individually, figure out how to curb violence? The last hundred years have been bloody, with several all-out wars, bitter civil strife pitting social or ethnic groups against each other, and the simple fact of more destructive weaponry. There have been many instances where several million people have been killed. Sophisticated explosives and delivery systems have allowed major states to visit massive attacks on other societies. But assault rifles and simpler bombs also did huge work in various kinds of civil conflict, where hundreds of thousands of people might die, sometimes even at the hands of child soldiers. And, although far less destructive, terrorist use of violence added to the general contemporary atmosphere in many specific regions. A blurring of lines between civilians and military personnel had occurred in some earlier periods in world history, as when armies attacked cities directly, but never with such devastating results as over the past several decades. Obviously, a host of international organizations have tried to curb these trends. Reports early in the twenty-first century claimed success in reducing the sheer number of conflicts. But it is impossible to predict where this aspect of contemporary world history will develop in the future – and, obviously, the issues are exceedingly important.

The list could easily be extended. In fact, it's not a silly exercise to think about major trends over recent decades that clearly are introducing change, but where a final statement about results cannot be issued. Not everything is up in the air: it's clear that the ratio of rural populations to urban (which dipped under 50% for the first time in world history, in 2009), will continue to decline. It's clear that a business-focused upper middle class will constitute the basic upper class in most societies around the world, replacing the aristocracy. It's clear that, for the foreseeable future, childhood will be defined primarily in terms of schooling. And these are important areas of contemporary change as well. But many vital topics can be framed, but not fully resolved – and this again contrasts with what historians can do, in hindsight, with every previous period.

(3) CULTURAL TRENDS

Cultural developments during the contemporary period are very difficult to characterize on a global level. Obvious and important trends include the steady advance of science and scientific discovery, and the increasing participation of societies outside the West in the modern scientific endeavor. International styles also emerged in art, particularly the visual arts and architecture; but not all regions in fact participated. The persistence of regional artistic traditions, either in resistance to or in combination with international trends forms an important comparative topic. For several societies also, the development of socialist-realistic styles was an interesting option for many decades.

The big challenge in the cultural area, however, involves balancing the continued roles of religion, including significant religious change, with competing belief systems. For some groups, intense nationalism might define a larger cultural outlook in some tension with religion. Even more widely, Marxist systems, either voluntarily adopted or enforced through a communist state, provided an alternative cultural framework. Marxism would largely disappear after 1990, in terms of organizing popular beliefs – an important and sometimes disorienting cultural development in its own right, but its role for many decades warrants attention. Most widely, in societies ranging from Japan to the West, some mixture of traditional values, consumer interests, and increasing reliance on science produced a largely secular cultural system that could have considerable force and that could link as well with globalization.

At the same time, however, religious commitments remained strong. Key groups retained traditional beliefs, and after the fall of European communism some interest in Orthodox Christianity revived in Russia. New missionary movements helped spread both Christianity and Islam in sub-Saharan Africa, which moved from being predominantly polytheist, in 1900, to largely Christian or Muslim (about 40% each) by 2000. More recently, evangelical Christian missionary movements have gained considerable success, particularly in Latin America. Most important of all – within Islam, Judaism, Hinduism, and Christianity – significant fundamentalist currents took shape particularly from the 1970s onward.

Contemporary world cultural history clearly involves not only regional diversity, on new as well as traditional bases, but also diversity and dispute within most regions. A great deal of change occurred, but in no single global direction. Recalling that, according to recent opinion polls, cultural globalization is the aspect most disliked by people around the world, as opposed to regional commitments, and the complexity of the cultural component of contemporary history becomes unavoidable.

(4) THE INTERWAR DECADES IN A CONTEMPORARY PERIOD

The final issue concerning the framework for contemporary world history involves the temptation to chop the last hundred years into smaller segments, rather than talk about a larger period at all, much less an open-ended one that is still taking shape. To be sure, all previous periods in world history have been at least more than a century long, and usually more than that. To turn to much smaller units for recent decades arguably changes the nature of the whole discussion. But there are no laws about periodization. Finer divisions in recent history may be not only justifiable, but very useful; and there's always the notion that the pace of change is speeding up anyway.

Some world historians isolate the war and depression decades, thus replacing any sense of the longer period of contemporary world history with a set of subdivisions. World War I unquestionably reflected and advanced a series of important issues, including the role of Germany. Its settlement did not resolve either the German question or the larger network of nationalist rivalries that could paralyze the continent. And the devastation of the war hampered constructive response. Several countries, with Japan the most important one, emerged frustrated and soon eager for new gains. The new communist regime in Russia created fears and hostilities. The United States, with its isolationist policy, pulled back from involvements. All of this added up to a recipe for disaster. The 1920s themselves, though superficially peaceful, saw increasing political polarization in many countries. New political movements, including Russian-inspired communism but also fascism, worked toward more authoritarian and repressive regimes. The Great Depression that started in 1929 partly resulted from the economic dislocations of the war. It caused a new round of suffering in many regions of the world, and helped fuel more desperate social and political movements, including military authoritarianism in Japan and Nazism in Germany. Several regimes were bent on war, and other powers were too weak or divided to stand in their way. Not only renewed world war, but unprecedented atrocities would result. Japan brutalized civilian populations in China. Soviet Russia, under Stalin, attacked real or imagined internal opponents, sending many to camps in Siberia and killing several million outright. Nazi Germany turned on the Jews, ultimately, after World War II broke out, slaughtering six million, in almost all parts of Europe, in the Holocaust. World War II itself brought even more massive casualties than its predecessor and, thanks to bombing raids by both sides, victimized large civilian populations in the process. Small wonder that many world histories pause over these three decades, under headings like "Decades of Crisis."

For the crisis did not fully persist after the war ended. The most barbaric contemporary political movements were discredited. A few semi-fascist or semi-Nazi groups persisted, not only in Europe but in Latin America, but they were rarely significant. This particular political innovation was largely snuffed out. Europe rebounded, setting up structures that reduced nationalist tensions and led to a real degree of continental unity, and reviving economic growth and popular cultural creativity as well. The Cold War was menacing, but in fact it produced few outright conflicts. After three decades bookended by massive wars, the decades since 1945 have been marked by regional, rather than general, outbreaks, sometimes quite intense but never engulfing the whole world. Decolonization and the economic surge of a number of regions outside the West both caused and reflected more positive developments than could be easily found in the earlier period of crisis. It becomes possible to focus on new trends, like the policies and technologies that supported globalization, or new problems, like environmental degradation, rather than the paralysis of the second quarter of the twentieth century.

Yet, most world history projects in fact talk about a contemporary era, usually beginning with World War I but occasionally a bit earlier. Of course they acknowledge world wars and depression, and specific but essentially short-term developments like fascism, but they also seek to identify some themes that transcend the divide between "crisis" and "post crisis" decades.

Here are some possible guidelines to this alternative approach, which sees a larger new period beginning early in the twentieth century:

- Important communications and transportation technologies advanced in the interwar years that enhanced global contacts, even in a challenging political and economic context. Further innovations would occur after World War II, when the policy environment for globalization would improve, but there are connections from the early twentieth century onward.
- Significant international political efforts also link between the interwar decades and what came later. The League of Nations, established after World War I, notoriously failed to prevent the conflicts that ultimately led to the second war, but it did provide patterns and examples that the later United Nations would build upon; and more focused groups, like the International Labor Office, formed in the early twentieth century but continued directly into more recent decades. Political globalization would accelerate, with key decisions about new global economic policy bodies after World War II along with the formation of the United Nations, but the process cuts across sub periods.
- Revolutions and the rise of nationalism in places like India and Africa both challenged traditional political forms like empires

and monarchies. This process clearly began with the great risings of the early twentieth century, including the Russian Revolution, and would continue after World War II. Many of the same developments, along with broader economic changes, promoted the decline of landed aristocracies and the rise of new business and managerial classes. Rates of urbanization continued to rise. Key social and political changes, in other words, stretch through the twentieth century and into the twenty-first.

- Women's rights: Changes in conditions for women unquestionably mark a process that runs through the whole contemporary period. Many societies, including Turkey and the Soviet Union as well as many Western nations, granted women the vote either shortly before or shortly after World War I; the process extended further after the second war. International efforts to promote women's rights moved forward between the wars but again would accelerate later.

- Population Explosion. The unprecedented increase in human population, that would propel a 300% growth in the twentieth century as a whole, runs through the entire contemporary period. The global spread of new public health measures, beginning to be installed in the later nineteenth century, most clearly explains the surge. But improvements in agriculture, most notably the "green revolution" of the 1970s, added in. The trend is not, however, neatly divisible within the twentieth century. Population growth contributed in some regions to new levels of poverty. It helps explain the twentieth-century push into cities, which in many societies now replaced the countryside as refuges for the poor. The growth would impel new patterns of international migration; some of these began to emerge first in the 1920s, with a movement of Algerian workers, for example, into France; the Depression and World War II did set this pattern back, with resumption only in the 1950s. Overall, however, population trends, which quietly but forcefully conditioned a host of contemporary global developments, need to be seen in terms of the longer span of time. Late in the twentieth century, and extending to the twenty-first, clear signs emerged of a global slowing in growth rates, and this will certainly shape key social developments later in the twenty-first century.

THE CONTEMPORARY PERIOD REVISITED

Granting the complexities of defining the contemporary period, dominant themes do exist. While the specific list will vary with any individual world historian, the themes do not have to be impossibly numerous: massive population growth, with migration, urbanization, and even environmental impacts is one clear area.

Accelerating globalization, with the underpinning of key changes in transportation and communication technologies but also important policy components, is a second. It's already been noted that a number of world historians believe that this category is not just a major new trend, but a real sea change in the framework of the whole human experience.

The movement to replace traditional staples of agricultural society, most notably monarchies, aristocracies, and full blown patriarchy, offers a third area. The theme advances through specific revolutions and nationalist movements, but it can be generalized. Cultural changes and resistances take shape partly in response to these trends as well.

Changes in the nature of warfare and violence might constitute a fourth trend area, embracing additional aspects of technology shifts but also the some of the deep nationalist, ethnic, and ideological tensions that have emerged during the past hundred years.

As in all previous periods in world history, the themes of the contemporary era must be used as a framework to encourage comparisons. Different societies have responded to major themes in different ways. Here is a vital way to test the interaction of regional continuities with the new patterns of the contemporary era, and to think in terms of the local/global tension and interchange.

Other comparative categories also make sense. A common one, which may reflect world economy precedents, involves distinctions in levels of economic development, between industrialized nations on the one hand, nations that are poorer and more agricultural on the other. Other terms for this division are North–South (because more of the developing societies are in the southern hemisphere) or "third world" for the less industrial group. Differences in economic position, linked to differences in life expectancy or education levels or other resource-based characteristics, must be kept in mind, even though the patterns shift over time.

Countries that have experienced revolution, versus countries that gained independence without revolution, constitute another interesting comparative category. Even though there have been no major revolutions for 30 years, the lingering effects of revolution on political, social and gender structure often differ from situations defined mainly by national independence movements. Still a third group of countries, mainly in the West, have not experienced either pattern during the past century, and sometimes have sought to defend conservative global policies to promote political stability as well as their economic interests.

A final comparative category, obvious from the earlier discussion of cultural change, involves comparing societies that maintain particularly active religious commitments, from societies whose cultures have become (or in some cases like China, have long been) more secular. Distinctions here involve not only beliefs and artistic patterns, but also definitions of the obligations of the state and degrees of tolerance, and even demographic and gender patterns.

In sum, experience with prior periodization provides guidelines for approaching contemporary world history. Beginning points should be discussed, major themes defined, and comparisons sketched. Possible comparative combinations expand however beyond the familiar civilization-to-civilization pattern, reflecting additional changes like the differential spread of industrialization or the selective experience of revolution. And, because the closing of the period cannot yet be pinpointed, the number of open-ended issues and potential debates is unusually vast.

FORECASTING

Contemporary history may, finally, blend into some efforts at prediction. This final component is not a uniform or essential part of world history, and many historians – nervous enough about dealing with current issues – shy away entirely.

Forecasting does flow from world history, and particularly contemporary history, in several key ways. Some forecasters rely heavily on analogy. Off and on, for example, since World War I, observers have claimed that Western society was in the process of declining as the Roman Empire did. This was a prediction based on claims of similarity to a known past event. Other analogies pop up recurrently. In 2009, for example, as the global financial crisis emerged, various people compared it to the Great Depression and tried to predict what might happen on that basis. The power of the Munich analogy, discussed in Chapter 3, continues strong (and many would argue, continues to mislead). Knowing when analogies are being used, and testing their historical validity, is an important asset in looking toward the future.

The most common forecast envisions at the future in terms of known current trends, which is where contemporary world history is particularly useful. Many scholars believe they know that icecaps will continue to melt because of global warming, causing new difficulties for coastal areas, on grounds that the developments have already begun. Only strong new environmental measures would modify the prediction. We also know that, because of low birth rates and increasing longevity, many populations will age over the next several decades, a process that has already started in Japan and most countries in the West and is beginning to emerge in China. How different the world will be with an unprecedentedly large percentage of people over 65 is anybody's guess, but the scenario is quite likely to be part of our future. And a final example: we know that China's economy has been growing very rapidly. Most experts assume that China will soon be one of the world's leading economic powers and that this will further shift power balances. Many forecasts see the roster of top economies by 2050 in terms of China, India, Brazil, the United States and (possibly) the European Union, believing that this captures the extension of patterns already underway.

Some forecasters sidestep both analogy and predicting on the basis of recent trends, trying to develop larger scenarios that might transform the world we live in. History, in this view, will contrast with the future, though contemporary history must also be explored to identify the seeds of transformation and the baseline for measuring change. Some environmentalists predict sweeping changes in the environment, along with population pressure on scarce resources that will alter, and worsen, the human condition. Globalization theorists, as we have seen, can argue not just that globalization is occurring, but that it will fundamentally change the ways societies operate reducing the usefulness of national units and governments, possibly obliterating the cultural identities we associate with civilizations. Another set of forecasts, under the heading of a postindustrial society, long contended that new technologies that automated production would reduce the need for workers and even conventional cities, creating a society with dramatically different work patterns and the need to figure out how to handle unprecedented amounts of leisure.

Forecasts that call for dramatic new scenarios can never be assessed fully, until the future actually arrives. Contemporary history does help, however, by showing whether there are at least some hints of a major shift and by helping to evaluate the claims over time. The postindustrial forecasts, for example, have faded in relevance for the moment because over the past decade or so the key issues in the global economy have been rather different from what the most extreme technology enthusiasts had projected.

The fact that we cannot actually know the future or fully assess some of the most dramatic scenarios brings us back one last time to the framework of contemporary world history. How much of the world today, or the trends that have shaped the past several decades, could have been reasonably predicted in 1900? Globalization perhaps, though its dimensions could not have been clear. The rebalancing of world powers was beginning to be glimpsed, or feared, but specific players like China would not have surfaced strongly. Virtually no one was anticipating the coming patterns of war and violence. The contemporary world, in sum, has taken shape on the strength of continuities from the past, trends that were beginning to emerge early in the twentieth century, but also a number of developments that could not have been anticipated at all. There's no reason to think that the next phase of contemporary world history will be any more fully predictable.

FURTHER READING

On important topics in contemporary history and globalization, see Ignacio Ramonet, *Wars of the 21st Century: New Threats, New Fears* (New York: Ocean Press, 2004); Makere Steward-Harawira, *The New Imperial Order: Indigenous responses to globalization* (London: Zed Books, 2005); Eric Hobsbawm with Antonio Polito, *On the Edge of the New Century* (New York: W.W. Norton & Company, 2001).

AFTERWORD

The rise of world history constitutes the most significant change in history teaching for the past half century, if not more. It follows from equally important changes in the world around us. It presses for clarity about how to handle time periods and the balance between change and continuity. It forces discussions of regional factors and comparisons, and their relationships to wide factors that shape the human experience. It organizes around an expanding list of core topics, with opportunities for further extension.

Above all, however, world history focuses on the changing dimensions of the tension between human separateness, created initially by the wider dispersion of the species, and the recurrent impact, and advantages, of contact and exchange. The tension emerged early, as local societies defined separate identities but also reached out through trade, war or migration. Greatly redefined, it continues to shape our world and complicate predictions even today.

It was in the fourteenth century that a Chinese observer, Wang Li, argued that interactions among peoples had become so extensive that "civilization has spread everywhere, and no more barriers existed. ... Brotherhood among peoples has certainly reached a new plane." World history helps explain why he could think that at the end of the Mongol period, but also why his vision proved misleading. Our own age sees observers proclaiming that intensities of contact mean that the world has become flat – even as others see a future defined ominously in terms of a clash of separate civilizations. The fundamental world history topic is constantly redefined, but it does not go away. The issue must clearly organize the vital effort to figure out how the global past has flowed into the global present.

GLOSSARY

Abolitionism movement or doctrine advocating the abolition of slavery

Agricultural revolution development of raising crops and animals as the major food source among human communities, replacing hunting and gathering

Analogy comparison based on shared features, allowing for further inference from the past

Aristocracy nobility; ruling class based on heredity

Artisan craftsperson; skilled worker practicing a specific trade or craft

Authoritarian system of leadership based on absolute obedience to a single ruler

BCE before the Common Era

Biological exchange process of plants, animals and often diseases being transferred from one region or society to another

Bronze Age period from 4000–1500 BCE; characterized by production of bronze tools and weapons

Buddhism religion, practiced primarily in Asia, based on the teachings and doctrine of Buddha, in particular the notion that human suffering will end with the cessation of desires

Bureaucracy system of nonelected government officials

Caliphate a leader of an Islamic jurisdiction; also the political system in the Middle East–North Africa in the postclassical period

Capitalism economic system based on private ownership, profit motive, and free trade

Caste system social structure in which social class and status are defined primarily by heredity

CE the Common Era

Christianity religion based on the teachings of Jesus and the belief that Jesus was the son of God

Chronology understanding based on the arrangement of events in time and the close study of dates

Civilization a complex form of human organization; a society defined by shared values and institutions

Class structure the organization of unequal social strata within a particular society

Classical period from 1000 BCE–500 CE characterized by expansion of key civilizations, integration of regional territory, and increase in regular interregional trade

Climate zone geographical region sharing a particular climate

Cold War period of political hostility between the USSR and its satellite states, and Western societies, particularly the United States, extending from 1945–91

Colonialism control of one country or society by another from afar; often implies exploitation of the smaller or less powerful country by the larger one

Columbian exchange   far-reaching transfer of plants, animals, humans (including slaves), diseases and cultural phenomena between the Eastern and Western hemispheres

Commercial agriculture   production of agricultural goods for sale

Commercialism   outlook in which commerce, business and trade take priority

Communism   system of social organization based on Marxist theories advocating the elimination of private property in favor of collective ownership

Confucianism   philosophy based on the teachings of Confucius, placing high value on devotion to family and ancestors, charitable outlook on humanity, education and political order

Consumerism   movement toward or value placed on increased consumption of goods

Constitution   fundamental law, set of laws or doctrine defining a government

Contemporary   period from 1914 on including rebalancing of world power/ decolonization, population explosion, globalization, replacement of agricultural institutions

Continuity   uninterrupted pattern, something that goes on or repeats without essential change

Core society   in world economy theory, a society exporting processed goods, profiting disproportionately from global trade

Crusades   religious military campaigns waged by European Christians in the Middle East between 1095 and 1291

Cultural history   interpretation of historical patterns or events based on popular culture, the arts, and other cultural trends among a group or groups of people

Culture   basic beliefs and assumptions, often also expressed in the arts

Decolonization   eliminating colonialism; freeing a colony from dependent status

Democracy   a government carried out by the people or representatives they have elected

Demography   the characteristics of a human population, or the study of these characteristics

Diplomacy   the practice of international relations; the development of relationships among different governments

Discipline   branch of knowledge or field of study

Dynasty   a succession of rulers from one family; the period of time defined by leadership of one such succession

Early modern period   1450–1750, rise of global trade, inclusion of the Americas, gunpowder empires

Economy   system of production, distribution and consumption of goods and/or services in a particular society or group of societies

Economic history   the study of the development of economies from an historical perspective

Emancipation   the act of freeing a person or group of people from the control of another

Empire   the domain ruled by an emperor or empress, often characterized by absolute power or authoritarian rule; sometimes involves territorial expansion

Environmentalism   concern with protecting the natural environment from pollution and other destructive forces

Epidemic   widespread outbreak of infectious disease

Evolution   genetic changes or developments in populations or societies over a period of time

Exchange   trade or transfer of goods, services and ideas within or among populations, cultures or societies

Expansion   the process of a territory or state growing, sometimes involving conquering another state; also refers to economic growth or recovery

Fascism   political theory advocating authoritarian and often totalitarian rule, hierarchical government system

Feminism   doctrine and political/social movements advocating equal rights for women

Feudalism   social and political system in post-classical Europe and Japan, based on land ownership by a ruling military class and relationships with vassals

Gender history   study of the past from the perspective of gender and gender conflicts

Global economy   interrelated and interdependent economies of the world

Globalization   the process of transforming local phenomena into global ones and intensifying interregional contacts

Government   organization or administration that is in charge of a political unit

Guerilla warfare   military initiatives taken on by individuals or organizations operating independently from a government

Gunpowder empire   empires, both land-based and overseas, in the early modern period based on use of guns

Habits of mind   dispositions of thought specific to a particular discipline and learning or study within that field

Hinduism   religion and philosophy predominant in the Indian subcontinent and some other parts of South Asia; characterized by beliefs in reincarnation, dharma, and a divine order that takes on various natures and forms

Hunter gatherer   society characterized by obtaining food via hunting and foraging; earliest form of human society

Immigration   migration into a new country or society

Imperialism   policy of extending rule or authority over another country or region

Individualism   philosophy or way of life advocating the primacy of the individual, individual rights and desires

Industrial Age   long nineteenth century plus contemporary period

Industrial revolution   transformation from agriculturally to industrially based societies

Infanticide   practice of killing newborn infants

Interdisciplinarity   the act of drawing from two or more distinct academic fields and the habits of mind they advocate

Internationalism   international in character or principle; doctrine advocating that nations should cooperate

Interwar years   the decades between 1918 and 1939

Iron Age   1500 BCE through 1450 CE, encompassing the Classical and Post-classical periods; but in some ways continues to the present

Islam   monotheistic religion predominant in North Africa and the Middle East and other parts of Asia and Africa, characterized by the belief in the teachings of the prophet Muhammed and the worship of Allah

Judaism   monotheistic religion based on the teachings of the Torah and Talmud

Kingdom   political or territorial unit ruled by a monarch or other sovereign

Kinship system   system of social relationships and often family characterizing a particular society

Laissez-faire   doctrine advocating individualism, particularly in the economic realm; the notion that government should not interfere in individual affairs

Leisure   time spent away from work

Local   relating to a particular place, city or town

Long nineteenth century   period from 1750–1914, characterized by industrial revolution, rise of Western power and imperialism, greater global economic inequality, emancipations

Marxism   theory based on the teachings of Karl Marx and Friedrich Engels, advocating the notion that all human behaviors and social developments have their basis in economics, and class struggle plays a central role in development

Merchant   businessperson engaged in buying and/or selling of goods

Migration   movement of people from one country or world region to another

Military   of or relating to warfare; system developed within a society for carrying out warfare

Missionary   a person, religion or philosophy aiming to convert others to a particular cause or belief system

Modern   usually assigned to periods since around 1700

Modernization   belief that various changes are linked in political function, education and technology; and that societies will change in similar directions

Monarchy   government run by a single leader (monarch) who may claim absolute rule; usually an inherited system of authority

Nation   group of people politically organized under a single government with explicit geographical boundaries, often claiming a distinctive culture and cultural coherence

Nation-state   political unit comprised of an autonomous state, populated by people who tend to share common culture and history

Nationalism   devotion to the interests and development of one's nation; often includes belief in the supremacy of one's nation over others

Neolithic Period (new Stone Age)   period from about 8000 BCE to 4000 BCE, characterized by agricultural revolution and rise of patriarchy

"New global historians"   historians arguing that recent globalization creates a dramatically novel historical context

"New nations" theory   idea that newly independent nations are often politically unstable because of internal conflicts, lack of experienced leadership and economic setbacks

Nomad   person or group of people with no defined home or territory; roaming lifestyle pattern, usually in a herding economy

Nongovernmental organization   organization characteristic of the contemporary period, operating independently of government and often without the goal of profit

Orthodox Christianity   form of Christianity prevalent in the Byzantine Empire, the Balkans and Russia; rift with Roman Catholicism in the 11th century

Parliament   legislative assembly participating in the government of a country and sometimes characterizing the governmental system

Patriarchy   system of social and/or familial organization based on the supremacy and centrality of the father or other males

Peasant   member of a social class comprised of farmers usually tightly tied to village structures

Periodization   the system historians use to define change and a resultant coherent set of trends, dividing chronology into periods

Peripheral society   in world economy theory, a society that exports cheap goods with exploited labor

Political history   historical understanding based on the analysis of diplomatic affairs, government forms and functions, events and dominant political theories and ideas

Political structure   system of government characterizing a specific region

Post-classical   period from about 600–1450 CE, characterized by spread of civilizations and world religions, rise of wider trans-regional trade networks, expansion of regional influences and imitations

Public health   science of and policy relating to preventing and curing disease and promoting health on a broad scale, societal and international level

Race   characterization of certain people based on inherited ethnic characteristics, often associated with skin color

Regime   political organization governing a society; government and rulers

Regional   characteristic of a specific place or geographical area

Religion   system of beliefs and rituals focused on ethics, a divine order, and the afterlife

Renaissance   period of European history from the fourteenth through mid-sixteenth century, defined particularly by new artistic styles

Revolution   drastic and far-reaching change, can be used to refer to either political or social changes of great magnitude; a revolution can also mean a violent uprising from below that seeks to alter political and social structures

River-valley civilization   early civilizations that developed along river banks, as in Egypt or Mesopotamia, primarily because of ease of irrigation and therefore agriculture

Science   systematic set of knowledge usually based on facts, truths or ideas that can be proven; usually focused on the workings of nature

Secular   not related to religion or spirituality

Settler societies   societies formed mainly by European settlers, as in the United States, Canada and Australia

Silk Roads   widely used trade routes established in the classical period, from China to the Middle East and Mediterranean

Slavery   bondage; human labor owned and controlled by other people usually without pay and sometimes characterized by inhumane treatment

Social history   explores the roles of ordinary people and a wide range of behaviors besides formal political behavior and intellectual life

Socialism   political theory calling for collective ownership of industry and government control over resources and services

Society   enduring social group whose members have organized patterns of interaction through trade, culture and/or politics

State   nation (or other political unit) or organized government

Syncretism   process in which beliefs or practices blend features from different groups or societies in contact

Technology   practical application of science to industry, knowledge or daily life

Terrorism   use of violence against individuals or a society for the achievement of religious or political goals

Third World   initially, countries like Egypt or India, not aligned with either side in the Cold War; came to mean poorer, economically developing regions. Not as widely used today

Topography   shape or features of an area of the Earth's surface

Trade   commercial exchange of goods and/or services

Tradition   long-standing custom; inherited pattern of thought or behavior

Trans-regional   comprising or relating to two or more regions and/or their relationships

Tribe   a social division or group of people, sometimes a family, who live or travel together

United Nations   political organization formed from a group of independent states in 1945 with the goal of promoting international peace and security

Urban   relating to a city or other area of dense population

Westernization   assimilation of or conversion to Western culture, values and belief systems

World economy theory   focuses on unequal global trade relations from the early modern period onward, and their long-term economic, political and social results

World war   a war involving most of the major nations of the world

Writing system   method for representing spoken language orthographically, using letters, signs or symbols

Zoroastrianism   system of religion founded in Persia in sixth century BCE, based on notion of struggle between good and evil

INDEX